STRANGERS IN CHAOTUI

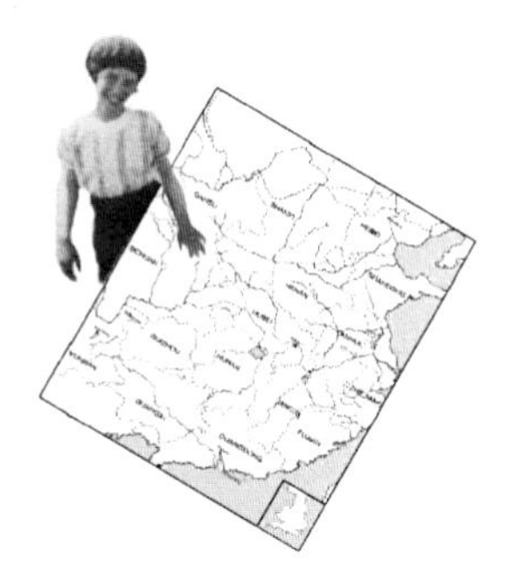

by Winifred Tovey

with letters and sections

by Frank Tovey

Published by

Little Knoll Press

Email: mail@littleknollpress.co.uk

Tel: 023 8084 2190

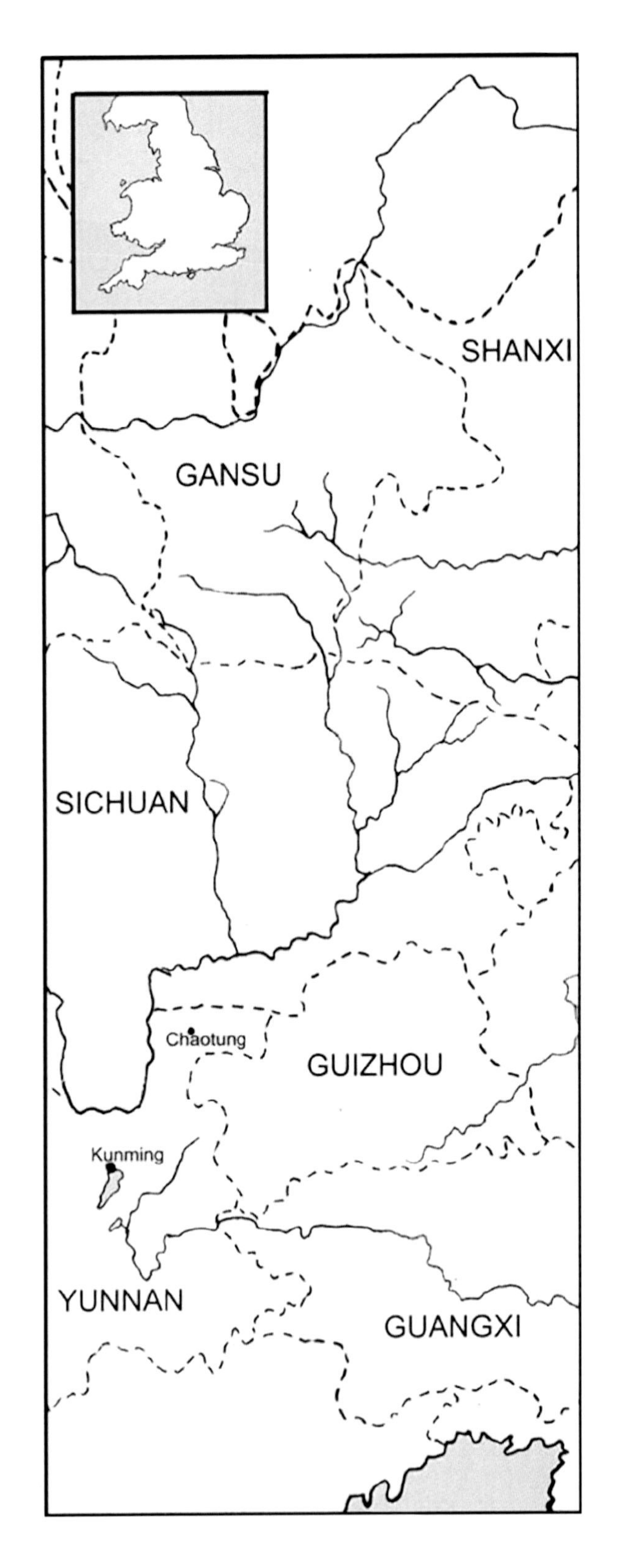

STRANGERS IN CHAOTUNG

by Winifred Tovey
with letters and sections
by Frank Tovey

Editing assistance by
Jenny Knowles (nee Tovey)

Published by
Little Knoll Press
Second imprint in 2010

Copies of this book can be obtained
by contacting
Little Knoll Press
Email: mail@littleknollpress.co.uk
Tel: 023 8084 2190

ISBN No. 978-0-9565359-0-0

Printed in Great Britain by the
MPG Books Group,
Bodmin and King's Lynn

STRANGERS IN CHAOTUNG

by Winifred Tovey, with letters and sections by Frank Tovey

Contents

CHINA - with provinces (spelt as in 1948) and scale map of England

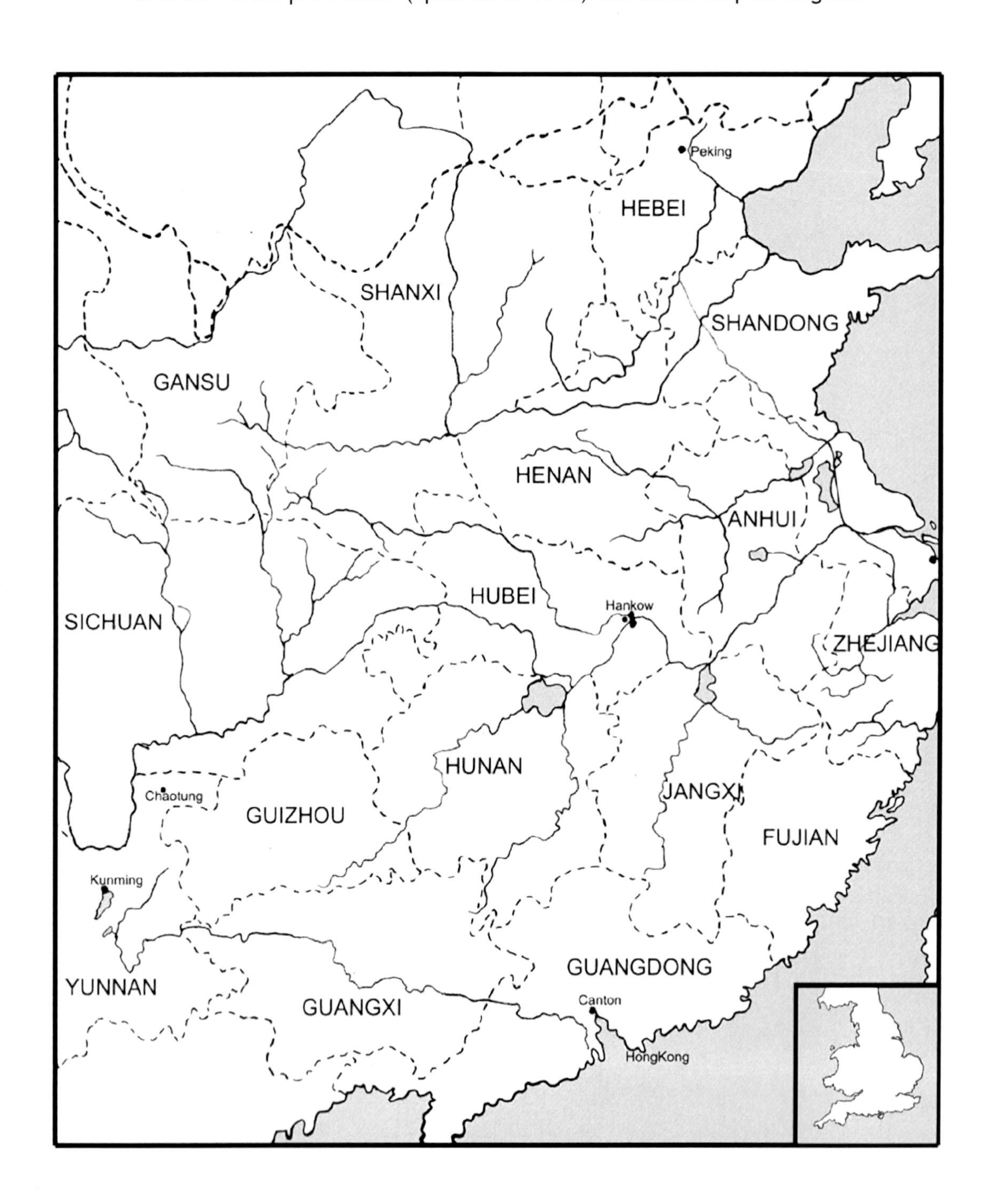

STRANGERS IN CHAOTUNG

Introduction

This story of a unique and fascinating beginning to sixty years of happy married life would have remained untold (for it is a vulnerable thing to contemplate opening personal letters to strangers) if it were not for the love and encouragement of our daughter, Jenny. It is with her dedication and enthusiasm that its publication has been achieved.

The story is of my husband, a surgeon, and myself, two ordinary people, with ordinary upbringings in England, who chose in 1947 to embark upon a journey that took us to work in a remote place in the heart of China. Our interest in foreign lands and missionary work had been stirred through magic lantern illustrated talks at our Methodist and Moravian churches, but in fact we knew very little about China when we set off on the long sea voyage. In preparation we had the experiences of childhood during hard times between two World Wars, and of several years of work during the Second World War in Britain, which had made us resilient and self-reliant. To our advantage, unlike the earlier pioneers, we would be living with colleagues at places where provision for the basic necessities of life was already established. Communication by post, although slow, was possible, and some roadways and bridges were in place in China, where before there had only been rough tracks. So it was that we left our families and our country with hope and excitement in our hearts.

We read some books about China on our sea voyage but we really only began to learn about the country when we arrived there, as you will understand when you read our story.

In order to give context to the time when we arrived in China I have included below a summary of the story told in the book 'Beyond the Clouds' by Elliot Kendall.

Summary of 'Beyond the Clouds'

In 1886 the 'Bible Christians' of the West Country (Cornwall and Devon) sent Thomas Thorne and Thomas Vanstone as the first missionaries to work in the North East region of the Province of Yunnan, China. A year later, Samuel Pollard and Frank Dymond, school friends from Shebbear School in Devon, joined them.

Sam Pollard and Thomas Vanstone were based in Kunming district, while Thorne and Dymond were in Chaotung. As customary with missionaries working in inland China in the 1800s, they wore Chinese garments and the men grew their hair long in Chinese queues. They endured great privations whilst travelling and ministering in their evangelistic work. Pollard was known for banging a gong and yelling himself hoarse, preaching using his rudimentary mastery of the Chinese language.

By 1890 Thorne had died, a new worker had also died before reaching Yunnan, and the Vanstones had been invalided home, with Vanstone seriously ill with malaria after their only child had died, and Mrs Vanstone a survivor of smallpox. Of the remaining missionaries, the only fit person was the newest recruit from Devon, Tremberth. Pollard was suffering constantly from malaria and stomach disturbances, and Dymond, who had survived smallpox, was exhausted.

Pollard then had the good fortune to meet and fall in love with Miss Hainge, a young lady of the China Inland Mission in Kunming. He travelled a thousand miles to marry her in Chungking, where there was a British Consulate.

The Pollards returned together to Chaotung to minister, but the city was not a friendly place, and the surrounding countryside was under the rule of warring barons, who used the rural population as serfs and slaves. Opium addiction, poverty, infanticide (particularly of girl babies), superstition, and shortage of food and safe water, added to the hardships of living in the high and remote, mountainous terrain. Against these odds Pollard and Dymond continued their work until 1900, when they had to retreat to French Indo-China during the Boxer Rebellion.

Before a year had gone by, Pollard returned to Chaotung, this time without his family, but carrying the additional attraction of magic lantern shows. Strapping the lantern onto his mule, he continued to minister to the people in the city and outlying district. In July 1904 an event happened that changed the history of the area forever. Four men from the Miao tribe arrived at Pollard's house. They had walked two hundred miles to find out more about the foreigner in their land, who always treated strangers with kindness, and who spoke of 'a god who loves us'. The Miao tribesmen described Pollard as 'of the same family, only come from a distance'.

In the following weeks and months Chaotung was inundated with visits from the Miao people, which caused the local Chaotung people some anxiety. Pollard decided to travel the mountains to the Miao villages. Here the landlords were disturbed by the influence that Pollard was having on the tribal people and they threatened to kill him, but he continued. Events took on their own momentum, and in December 1904 four thousand Miao arrived in Chaotung to hear the Christmas story.

In 1905, ten acres of land in the mountains was gifted, to provide the site for a church, school and clinic for the Christian work. This place, a good day's journey from Chaotung, was known locally as 'Shi-men-k'an' (or The Stone Threshold'), and became, by rough translation, 'Stone Gateway'. Pollard moved out of Chaotung to live with the Miao in Stone Gateway.

The work and lives of all foreigners and of the Chinese people, Han and tribal, who were perceived to sympathise with Christianity, were very precarious, and in the early years of Stone Gateway, the Miao ministers and Pollard were pulled from their homes and beaten near to death. Pollard was joined at Stone Gateway by a number of colleagues, including the parents of Ken and Keith Parsons (Ken drove us from Kunming to Chaotung in 1948).

From 1911 the advent of Christianity in Kunming was visibly more accepted. At Stone Gateway the Christian community was strong, but still subject to epidemics, such as the typhoid that took Pollard's life in 1915.

Samuel Pollard's story, although remarkable, reflects the unassuming attitude of the foreigners who pioneered work in China. They accepted social and political instability without remark.

When we travelled to China, most of Yunnan was still remote and therefore still lagged behind the East of China in terms of news and events. The northern Yunnan terrain was difficult and the rewards of invasion few. Most unrest was still caused by the age-old, and local, power struggles between warlords, tribal peoples and the growing population of Han Chinese.

After the Boxer Rebellion, the Revolution of 1912 resulted in the establishment of the Chinese Republic and a period of social stability. But it was short-lived and a power struggle between the Chinese Nationalists and Communists developed. This was further complicated by the Japanese invasion during World War 2. The Japanese captured many missionaries, and the Inland China Mission withdrew most of its staff from the country.

Frank and I arrived in China, fresh from England, alongside the missionaries who were returning after the furlough that followed their internment by the Japanese.

Now, read on with sympathy, as I relate some memories of my childhood and growing up, meeting Frank and our whirlwind marriage, and then share with Frank the tale of our journey to China and the adventures that we experienced in the eighteen months that we lived in that unknown country.

1919 to 1935

My earliest real memory is of my father, Frederick Hill, when he returned home from work in the evening just about my bedtime and we would spend a few minutes together. I remember clambering up onto his knees and together we would chant, 'Ride a cock-horse to Banbury Cross, To see a fine lady ride on a white horse, With rings on her fingers and bells on her toes, She shall have music wherever she goes'. At the same time Daddy would be jogging me up and down as if I was on the horse. How I enjoyed that ride! I always wanted more, as small children do, but eventually Daddy would carry me upstairs to bed. I must have been about two and a half years old at the time.

My mother, Nellie Louise, was seventeen or eighteen years old when she married Frederick Hill in 1914 or 1915, and my father was twelve years older than her.

I have just this one photograph of my parents, which I think could have been their marriage photograph. My father looks a quiet, aesthetic kind of person. He was artistic and worked for the local newspaper engraving illustrations. He was also an oboe player and a smoker. Mother kept his oboe and pipes for many years after his death.

I can still picture the pipes hanging in their rack on the wall. They were long and bent into an S shape, exactly like the pipes smoked by Sherlock Holmes in films.

My brother, Arthur, was born on November 5th 1916. My father must have been called up quite early in the First World War and have married Mother before going to fight. He served with the Horse Artillery in the trenches, and in the battle of the Somme, for three years or more. I visited the area some years ago and saw a film depicting the conditions of the time. I can only imagine the mud, cold and noise of distressed horses struggling to haul gun carriers through the churning mud amidst the roar of gunfire and battle. It must have been horrendous. Mother later told me that when father arrived home on leave from the battlefront he would not enter the house until he had removed all his clothing and washed down in the garden shed. This was to remove both the mud and lice.

I was born in September 1919 and apart from the one early memory, I have no clear recollection of my father. Many years later, I learnt that father had suffered from chronic nephritis from the time when he came back home. He must also have been very depressed by the whole wartime experience. He died suddenly in 1924. I do not know how or when exactly, but I have a niggling memory of children calling after Arthur and me in the street, shouting something about 'putting his head in the gas oven'. Mother never spoke about this to me and Arthur told me to 'take no notice of the horrible children'.

I think it is likely that Father suffered from what is now called post-traumatic shock. He had come back to England in the Great Depression, and at a time when there was little effective treatment for chronic nephritis, and its progress, although slow, was relentless. I also wonder whether, as a five year old, I was deeply upset at losing a beloved Daddy, and the family wanted to protect me by ignoring the whole episode. This may well account for the almost complete blank in my mind concerning events prior to his death.

I will now take up the story from 1924, when Mother, then aged twenty seven, was left to care for my brother, aged eight, and me, aged five, on a widow's pension of five shillings a week. The first thing she did was to sell our house. It was a semi-detached, fairly new building with a bathroom fitted with a gas geyser for hot water, a separate toilet and three bedrooms upstairs, and downstairs a front parlour, dining room, living room and kitchen. Outside, at the back of the house, there was a second toilet, a coal barn and a good-sized garden. With the proceeds from this sale Mother purchased a small grocery store and we moved to live with her parents.

Arthur and I pose for a studio photograph in 1924.

I think this must have been before our father's death and the stringent circumstances that forced Mother to take us to live in Granny and Grandpa Edwards' house.

Mother was one of eight siblings (six boys and two girls). The oldest was William, next Stanley, then Frederick, followed by Mother (Nellie), Harold, Cyril, George and the youngest, Gladys. George and Gladys were then aged seventeen and fifteen respectively, and still living in the family home when we three joined them. I found it difficult to understand why Gladys was so upset by our intrusion, but of course, after fifteen years as the youngest child in a large family, her special status was suddenly usurped, and to add insult to injury, my mother and I were suddenly sharing her bedroom.

Granny and Grandpa's house was quite small. It was one of a terrace in the town of Bedford, with three bedrooms upstairs. Downstairs was a front parlour with a bay window, where the aspidistra had pride of place, a central living room fitted with a coal fired cooking range, and a large scullery with a flagstone floor and built-in copper in one corner. Next to the copper was a huge stone sink with one coldwater tap that served the whole house. On the other side of the scullery was Granny's pride and joy - a gas cooker. A good-sized walk-in pantry opened off the scullery and boasted a beautiful, cool, long, black marble shelf, which was a great luxury for storing perishable foods on warm summer days.

Through another door a large coal barn stored the coal, brushes, brooms, dusters, polish, buckets, a large zinc bathtub and one other most important item Grandpa's weekly ration of Gorgonzola cheese. Granny refused to allow this in the pantry because she said she 'just could not bear its potent smell'.

This small house, that a family of ten had been living in, had just one lavatory, situated outside in a little, lean-to, brick building behind the kitchen. It had a flush toilet, and during cold winter nights we had to keep a candle burning under the water pipe that fed the cistern to prevent the water from freezing. It was dark and damp, so our visits to this 'little room' on a cold winter day would be very quick.

A wooden garden shed stood just behind the lavatory wall, large enough for all the garden tools and our bicycles. Walking and cycling were our main means of transport to work and school.

The garden was a little wider than the house building and stretched for about twenty-five yards behind the house. A small path ran down the centre of the plot. On one side we grew tidy rows of peas, runner beans, carrots, cabbages and beetroot, and on the other side were sweet peas, cosmos, sunflowers, pansies, dahlias and roses, randomly planted and providing a riot of colour and fragrance.

When our two households became one, careful thought was given to sleeping arrangements, and after much deliberation it was decided that George and Arthur would share the small back bedroom, Granny and Grandpa the middle bedroom, and Gladys, Mother and I the front bedroom. Poor Gladys, I am not surprised that she was resentful at first. Fifteen years old is a difficult age at which to lose your privacy.

On arising in the morning Grandpa, George and Arthur would wash and shave at the sink in the scullery, whilst we 'ladies' washed upstairs. There was a washstand for Granny, and another for mother, Gladys and me. The washstands each held soap, a large ewer of cold water and a large bowl. Below we kept a bucket, into which we poured the dirty water, which we carried downstairs for disposal. One by one we would scramble out of bed and take our turn pouring a little water into the bowl and washing as quickly as possible. During the coldest winter weather our wash would often be a 'lick and a promise'.

The house was unheated apart from the kitchen range, and getting out of a warm bed was a miserable shivery business. Often, overnight, ice would form over the water in the ewer and Jack Frost would leave beautiful, frosty patterns on the windowpanes. I would pull my daytime clothes inside my warm bed and wriggle around under the bedclothes changing from night to daytime underclothes before washing.

For years after the First World War there was great hardship. Thousands of people had no work and money was extremely scarce. My wardrobe consisted of school uniform, which for the winter months consisted of a liberty bodice (an undergarment made from thick or quilted cotton), a pair of bloomers (described in the dictionary as 'women's loose-fitting, knee-length knickers'), black Lisle stockings, black lace-up shoes, navy gymslip, white blouse, pullover, a navy Gabardine, full length raincoat and a black felt, brimmed hat. Summer uniform was much lighter: a cotton vest, cotton knickers, short white cotton socks, black lace-up shoes, quite smart cotton dresses in blue and white gingham, a cardigan and navy blazer. Mother would usually keep back the newest set of uniform for Sunday wear, and, needless to say, the older uniform would be worn for play. Gymslips were quite expensive but they were designed to last for years and years. The necks were square and fastened at the shoulder by two buttons on each side. Mother would alter the shoulder straps to button with a wide overlap when the garment was new, then as I grew in height, the buttons would be moved to make the garment longer. Also, the original hem would be three or four inches deep, so as the years went by it could be let down. The worst problem when clothing young children on a very limited budget was shoes; even if they were too big when first bought, we outgrew them before they were worn out. My feet suffered quite badly from wearing shoes that were considered too good to replace but were too tight for my growing feet.

Arthur and me in Brighton in 1927
on a Sunday School outing from
Bedford.
I have my dress tucked into my
'bloomers' in this photo.

I remember when Grandpa agreed to have 'new-fangled' gas supplied to the house. A gas cooker was installed and Grandpa allowed Granny to have a gas fire fitted in her bedroom and one gas light point in the kitchen. For other light we continued to use oil lamps and candles. During our schooldays, in the evening, Arthur and I were banished to the front parlour to do our homework. A satisfactory enough arrangement throughout the warm spring and summer months, but when winter arrived, it could be very uncomfortable. Huddled into our warmest winter clothing, including hats and scarves, we would sit, one each side of a small table, working by the light of an oil lamp. One consolation was that the oil lamp gave a warm and cosy glow to the room.

Our schoolwork did not seem to suffer unduly, and we both managed to reach the highest grades on leaving school at the age of sixteen. Our schooldays were in the years of the great depression when money was extremely short, and a coal fire was only lit in the parlour during the Christmas season. All our friends and neighbours were in the same predicament and we made the best of life as we knew it.

My Grandmother worked extremely hard. She ran the house like clockwork. Each day of the week had a particular list of 'jobs to be done'. Monday was washday and Granny would be up at 6a.m. with the copper to be filled with cold water and coal fire to be lit. While the water was heating up, she prepared the family breakfast, usually a bowl of porridge each. Around 8.30a.m, when we had all departed for school or work, Granny would add soap and soda to the hot water in the copper, pile in the first load of clothes, cover the lot with a large wooden lid and leave it to boil whilst she prepared our lunch. Grandpa, Arthur and I always returned home for lunch. Once the final load of washing was completed, Granny drained the hot water from the copper through a tap situated low down on its side, before rinsing the washing in clean, cold water in the sink.

I particularly enjoyed coming home from school and helping Granny put freshly washed laundry through the huge mangle. It was satisfying to fold the dripping sheets, towels and shirts, place them between the rollers and turn the big handle to see them come out on the other side squashed flat and ready to hang on the washing line in the garden to dry. The zinc bathtub placed underneath the mangle rollers caught the excess water squeezed from the garments. After drying, sheets and pillowcases were very carefully folded and passed through the mangle a second time. This greatly reduced the amount of ironing required.

Tuesday, if the washing had dried, was ironing day. Granny spread a large, old, folded blanket on the plain wooden kitchen table, and covered it with a cotton sheet. Heavy flatirons were heated on the gas ring, one left on the ring getting hot whilst the other, already heated, was being used. The irons were really heavy and only adults were allowed to use them. Great care had to be taken when testing the temperature of the irons. Granny taught me to lick my middle finger and quickly touch the surface. If a small hissing sound could be heard the temperature was just right, but if there was too little moisture on your finger you could easily burn your skin. Washing and ironing for seven people was very heavy work and I often wonder how Granny managed to do it all after already having raised a family of eight.

Wednesday and Thursday were dedicated to house cleaning and shopping. During the week, bread, milk, greengroceries, and coal were all brought door to door around the streets by horse and cart. The butcher's shop was just around the corner, as was a wonderful fish and chip shop. There was nothing more appetising than a 'pen'orth' of chips on a cold winter day.

On Friday afternoon, the end of the working week, Granny filled the copper with water once again and lit the coal fire beneath. While the water was heating, my job was to sit on the kitchen step with a long row of shoes spread out before me, one pair for each member of the household. Then, with polish and brushes at the ready, I had to polish every pair, even my brother's.

Many a time I felt really cross about this. I would sit, brush in hand, lips pursed, vigorously brushing and muttering, 'Why should I clean Arthur's shoes? Its not fair.'

Seven pairs of shoes was certainly a challenge. Sometimes, if I was in a particularly grumpy mood, Grandpa would say, 'Use a little elbow grease child, that will bring up the shine.' As the years passed, I learnt the truth of this remark and took great pride in lining up a row of beautiful, sparkling shoes ready for wearing to church on the Sunday morning.

The redeeming feature about this shoe-cleaning chore was being in the right place to watch Grandpa as he carried out a very skilful weekly task of sharpening his razors. It never ceased to fascinate me. Hanging from a hook fixed to the back of the scullery door was a long leather strop. Every Friday evening, Grandpa took the lower end of the strop in his left hand and proceeded to sharpen his two cutthroat razors. Holding them, one at a time, in his right hand he would spend between fifteen and twenty minutes lovingly 'stroking' each razor up and down the strop, pausing from time to time, to test the blade against the ball of his thumb, until he was happy that it had reached a satisfactory degree of sharpness.

Watching this display of skill was restful and certainly helped me shine the shoes, in fact I probably brushed the shoes in time with his sharpening strokes. I never ceased to ask him, 'Grandpa, how do you manage to actually shave with such a sharp blade without cutting your chin?' I cannot remember ever seeing him walking around with a patch of plaster on his chin.

On Friday evening, following these important activities, the zinc bathtub was brought from the coal barn and placed on the floor in the centre of the scullery. Soap and towels were laid out alongside, the curtain was drawn across the window above the sink and the back door locked. Hot water was then drawn through the copper tap into a bucket, carried across and tipped into the bathtub, then cold water would be drawn from the tap and added to the copper to heat in readiness for other members of the family to use later. Granny, followed by Grandpa, took their baths.

Grandpa worked as a foreman in W. H. Allen's Iron and Steel Works, which stood alongside the railway station just ten minutes' walk from our house. His working day began at 7.30a.m. and ended at 5p.m. with one hour break for lunch. Living so close, he always came home for the midday meal. As a foreman, he did not get unduly dirty at work, although a lot of very fine dust always seemed to collect in his hair and clothing. I imagine after the noise and clamour of the factory all week he must have treasured his weekly bath, with the long soak in warm water, and then the blissful feeling of fresh, clean underclothes and shirt against the skin. Mind you, after the relaxation came the task of emptying the dirty bath water down the kitchen sink, then refilling the bathtub with clean hot water from the copper in readiness for the rest of us.

I shared the bath with my Mother. When finished we would wrap ourselves up, each in a large, dry towel, and scuttle quickly upstairs to dry off, don our nightclothes and hop into bed. In this way we managed to give Arthur time to bathe on his own. He used our bath water freshened up with a little extra hot water from the copper. (As I grew older I took my bath separately.) After Arthur's bath the dirty water was emptied away and fresh water heated in the copper for Gladys and George to use later in the evening.

Fortunately, the bath water did not become very dirty. We were aware of the great need to be thrifty and willingly accepted whatever steps Granny wished to impose upon us to make 'ends meet'. This kind of economy was practised in thousands of households throughout the 1920s and 30s. The whole process was extremely laborious because the dirty water had to be disposed of by bailing it out of the bath into a bucket, then either poured down the sink or, during the summer, used to water the plants in the garden. During the coldest weather we always looked forward to bath night, as the copper fire warmed the scullery.

Saturday arrived, and for Arthur and me this usually meant helping Mother in the shop. Occasionally Mother would give us a 'day off' to play with friends or go into town and look around Woolworth's, Sainsbury's or Marks and Spencer's, mostly window shopping.

Sunday was always a 'day of rest'. The whole family, Grandparents, George, Gladys, Mother, Arthur and I, together walked the short distance to Church for 10.30 morning service. We always sat together along the same pew. For some years, when Arthur and I were quite young, the resident minister was a very enthusiastic, demonstrative preacher who emphasised every point by gesticulating wildly. Arthur and I usually sat next to each other and, as children will, we giggled whenever he became particularly 'wild'. Mother would tolerate this behaviour for a while, but eventually, with a severe look, she would separate us for the remainder of the service.

This photo is of
Granny and Grandpa Edwards
in about 1934.

It is a little later than the times described on this page, but I have put it here so that you can picture how they looked.

After service we returned home to a roast beef lunch. The meat and vegetables were prepared on Saturday evening, and before church on Sunday morning Granny would stoke up the kitchen range fire and place the meat, potatoes, parsnips and carrots into the oven to roast while we were at church. We all enjoyed a leisurely

Sunday lunch and lingered at the table afterwards to watch Grandpa partake of his precious Gorgonzola cheese, complete with its maggots. 'All part of the cheese', he would say in answer to my 'yukki' remarks about the wriggly maggots. Following this wonderful lunch the grownups usually settled down for an afternoon nap, while Arthur and I were sent off to Sunday School for an hour. We returned home for a cup of tea and then went back to church with the rest of the family for the 6.30pm service.

Born and nurtured within the heart of a Christian family, on both paternal and maternal side, I found no difficulty in believing in God and Jesus. Reading the bible, thanking God for our food every day, praying for those less fortunate than ourselves, asking for forgiveness for any wrong that we might have done, was all part of the fabric of daily living. In Sunday School we heard the parables and teachings of Christ, and as we grew older we read the Acts of the Apostles. Paul's journeys particularly stirred my imagination. Why should I doubt that they were true? At the age of fifteen I was confirmed into the membership of the Moravian Church. It was the impact of St. Paul's journeys that planted in my mind the longing to go abroad to help ease the lives of those less fortunate than myself. I was never to experience a 'sudden conversion' as happens for some people.

It was through Church services, with their tuneful hymns, that I also developed my love for singing and music. I am not sure exactly how, or when, but a piano found its way into Granny's kitchen. Mother possibly brought it from our home, because I know Arthur was taking piano lessons there before our father's sudden demise.

At that time, 1924, young children often were not directly informed about a sudden death in the family. It was assumed that they were too young to understand such things. We were told, 'Daddy has gone away for a while and we are moving to live with Granny Edwards.' The whole family did their best to make our transition into the new way of life easy and we just accepted that sometime Daddy would come back. I cannot remember exactly when I realised he would never return, but I think that living in a busy household made it easier to cope with his absence because there was no time to sit and brood. Grandpa's favourite remark to me was, 'Don't sit there idly dreaming, child. Get up and help your Granny.'

During the years 1924 to 1929, the piano stood in Granny's kitchen and Arthur and I received lessons and passed Trinity College examinations. I was particularly fond of the tune, 'The Swallows Return'. Day after day, upon arriving home from school in the afternoon, I would play it, over and over again, partly because I enjoyed the tune, but also in order to perfect my fingering and timing. Poor Grandpa would come home tired after a long, hard day at work, to find me in the kitchen tinkering away at this very monotonous little tune. 'Can't you find another tune, child?' he would say. All he wanted to do was sit by the warm fire in the kitchen, smoke his pipe, and quietly enjoy a cup of tea.

In 1929, my tenth year, my piano teacher put my name forward to compete in the local Eisteddfod. The great day came and I left home alone just after breakfast, to arrive at the Corn Exchange and join the throng of other contestants. I cannot remember how many there were, but, when my turn came, I remember walking between the curtains and onto the stage, in the middle of which stood a piano stool and a beautiful, dark, shiny, grand piano. The hall looked huge and I felt so small. Looking across from the platform into the body of the hall I could just make out the black silhouette of a row of seated people, the Adjudicators. Timidly, I perched on the piano stool and played my piece. Performance over, I left the stage as quietly as I had walked on, and with no idea what to do next, I made my way back to the waiting room and sat down. From time to time a name would be called and the named child would walk away to disappear through the curtain on to the stage. After a few minutes a tearful child would appear back among us, then quickly leave for home. By the end of the day just sixteen of us were left waiting. We, the chosen few, were told to return to the Corn Exchange at ten o'clock the next morning for the final selection. Tomorrow was to be the FINALS and I was one of the final sixteen hopefuls.

I remember skipping all the way home with the excitement of it, only to be brought swiftly back to earth with a stern reprimand for causing so much anxiety by staying out so late. I had arrived back home at 7.30 in the evening and my Grandparents and Mother were very angry. I was upset that they found it so hard to believe that I really had reached the finals, and went to bed crying with tiredness and disappointment.

Next morning, alone once more, I set off for the Corn Exchange, Grandpa's parting remark still ringing in my ear, 'Don't be so late home tonight. You should know better than to give your Mother so much anxiety.'

On reaching the Corn Exchange for the second morning in a row, this time with fifteen other candidates, I soon began to chat and relax. We went through the same procedure as the day before, until by process of elimination just three of us were left and, to my amazement, I was one of the three. We were Gold, Silver and Bronze Medal winners, and I had won the Silver Medal. All my hard work had not been in vain. I rushed home bursting with pride, and crashed through the scullery door crying, 'I've won, I've won, I've won the silver medal', only to be met with disbelief and incredulity. My bubble was burst.

Of course, in the end, the good news did sink in, and my Mother, bless her, rushed out and bought a length of pale green silk, which she made into a lovely dress for me to wear at the presentation ceremony. On the day she actually closed the shop and joined me at the Corn Exchange for the presentation.

Sadly, all my certificates and the silver medal were mislaid later when a trunk, left behind in Ockbrook Moravian Settlement, near Derby, whilst we were in India, went missing and was never found.

Just after this memorable occasion my piano playing career abruptly ended. Throughout my earlier childhood I had recurrent attacks of tonsillitis, as well as the usual infections of measles, chicken pox and scarlet fever. My tonsils and adenoids were removed at one stage but still the high temperatures recurred. Eventually it was thought that I had 'TB Tummy' and the doctors ordered 'complete rest for one year, no school and as much rest as possible'. Sadly, the piano disappeared from the house because Mother thought I was 'playing too much and wearing myself out'.

After that neither Arthur nor I had access to any instrument for many years. As we grew older we both continued to nurture our love of music by taking part in concerts organised by The Young People's Society within the Church fellowship. We were twenty-five to thirty in number and often performed musical items. One incident I shall never forget was when Arthur was acting the barber and I his client. Dressed for the part we began to enact a client coming for a haircut and shave. All went well, with both of us singing away gustily during the hair cutting stage but when it came to placing the cloth around my neck ready for shaving, Arthur, in his enthusiasm, accidentally knocked his hand against my 'Adam's apple', causing my voice, in the middle of a particularly loud, high note, to wobble in the most alarming way. The whole audience was reduced to laughter, the actors likewise. We did eventually finish the skit to loud and prolonged applause.

To return to our younger years, we regularly sang in the church choir on Sundays and one of our tasks was to take turns at pumping the church organ during services. It was a beautiful, two manual pipe organ, fitted with a hand pump placed behind a curtain to one side of the organ. The pumping action was quite hard work and two of us needed to sit behind the curtain and take turns. Occasionally, the organist got carried away with enthusiasm when playing an uplifting piece of music, causing the organ to demand extra air, and as the bellows began to run out of air, the music would slur and sigh, creating an alarming situation for the organist. We children, of course, thought this was hilarious and, although we tried our best to keep up the pressure, just occasionally, for fun we would deliberately pump more slowly.

My Mother's prudent decision to purchase a small grocery store meant that from 1924 to about 1936, throughout our schooldays, she was able to contribute a considerable amount towards the household budget. Arthur and I gladly spent our Saturdays in the shop. My job was to weigh biscuits, sugar and various commodities and make up customers' orders, and Arthur's job was to ride around on his bicycle delivering the orders. We thoroughly enjoyed doing this and made friends with many of Mother's regulars. The butcher, who owned the shop next door, became a very good friend. Often, during a quiet time of the day, I would go round to watch him make sausages, gathering up the string as they left the machine. I expect I must have looked thin and hungry, as occasionally he would put a few sausages into a paper bag and give them to me, saying, 'There you are love, take them home and have them for supper.'

Such favours were often passed on. After closing time on Saturday evenings I would always be sent across the road to take a basket of provisions to mother's elder brother, Uncle Will, who lived with his wife and two children in a flat opposite the shop. Uncle Will had contracted tuberculosis when serving in the army during the war and was unable to work.

During our schooldays Arthur and I spent three or four summer holidays at Potten End, near Berkhamstead, with Granny Hill, my father's mother. When this plan was first mentioned I was nine years old and Arthur twelve. The only way of reaching Potten End was to cycle. The whole idea of spending time on a farm sounded exciting and I could not bear the thought of Arthur going away without me. What could I do? 'I know', I said, 'I will try to earn a little doing odd jobs and I'll save all my pocket money then I shall have enough money to buy a second-hand bicycle.'

When February came, Arthur and I set off one day for the cattle market, my money safely stowed deep in my coat pocket. This market was one of our favourite haunts when visiting Bedford town. We would spend hours looking around at the cows, pigs, sheep, chickens, kittens, puppies and rabbits. Surrounding the cattle market were stalls where second-hand bicycles could be found, and on this particular day I had only one thing on my mind. After very careful inspection of all the old bicycles available, Arthur selected the one he considered suitable for me, his little sister, and began haggling for the price. Eventually I successfully purchased a second-hand, upright, Raleigh bicycle for the princely sum of £2. I could not yet actually ride a bicycle, so I pushed it all the way home. I was so proud of my purchase.

Uncle George kindly turned the bike over so that it stood resting on its handlebars and saddle. This, he said, was the ideal position from which to carry out my oiling, polishing and general smartening up operation before embarking upon my first ride. Luckily, it did not take me long to gain confidence and after a few short trial runs I was ready for anything.

A day or two before our departure for the long awaited summer holiday, our summer clothing, towels and toiletries were packed into two small cases and securely strapped onto the racks fitted above the rear wheel guards of the bicycles. Then, early in the morning, with a few sandwiches and a bottle of juice, our 30-mile ride to Potten End began, travelling by way of Ampthill, past Whipsnade Zoo and on to the village of Potten End. I remember, on one occasion near Whipsnade we caught a glimpse of a giraffe in the distance, and hoping to see more exotic animals, we sat down on the roadside to eat our sandwiches. It was a beautiful deserted spot with a wonderful view across the rolling hillside. The only sounds to be heard were sheep bleating and birds singing. It was very peaceful and we enjoyed a well-earned rest, but we did not see any more of the zoo animals.

The journey took four hours or more to complete, a shorter time as we grew older, and was a great adventure, it being highly unusual for two children of our ages to cycle so far away into the countryside alone. On a fine summer day, for most of the time, we would be riding along quiet, narrow roads between hedgerows. At first the landscape was fairly flat, then as we approached Ampthill we met the first steep hill. Beyond this point we encountered a lovely area of rolling countryside, passing woodlands and farms, and near Whipsnade Zoo we cycled over the Chiltern Hills. None of it was too strenuous and the roads were practically empty of traffic, there being no cars or huge lorries to disturb the peace, only an occasional horse and cart or a farmer taking his sheep or cattle from one field to another. We would safely reach Potten End in time for tea.

Granny Hill was a sweet little lady. I can still picture her standing to greet us at the door of her cottage, neat in her black dress with its long, full skirt and tight-fitting bodice, always adorned with a dainty, white lace collar, and her head crowned with a white lace cap. She wore dainty, black leather boots, the legs reaching up to her knees. Often she would give me the task of buttoning or unbuttoning the row of tiny buttons, which ran all the way, from ankle to knee, up the outer side of each bootleg. I felt it was a great honour to be allowed to use the hook made especially for this purpose. When walking out of doors she wore a black bonnet decorated with sequins and fastened under the chin with a bow of black ribbon.

Granny lived in a tiny, cosy, thatched cottage. Arthur and I slept in two small bedrooms, each with a sloping ceiling and a small window opening under the overhang of the thatched roof. It was very snug. Behind the cottage was a garden filled with flowers, a couple of apple trees, a few gooseberry, black and redcurrant bushes and a row each of raspberry canes, peas and runner beans.

The privy was hidden behind the gooseberry bushes. It was a wooden structure, rather like a garden shed, built over a very large, deep, septic tank, with wooden seating above, consisting of two wide planks set at slightly different heights, one for children and one for adults. I was quite nervous visiting the privy, because among the roof timbers of the small building there were cobwebs hanging, and, just as I got seated, I would spot huge spiders moving around above my head. As a ten year old I did not waste much time in this little 'house'. But this was really a minor inconvenience. Our holidays with Granny Hill were so full of sunshine, fun and interest, and I would not have missed them for the world.

Our days were spent helping Uncle Charles (Granny Hill's brother-in-law) and Auntie Margaret on their small farm in Potten End, less than half a mile away from Granny Hill's. After breakfast Arthur and I would walk to the farm and spend the rest of the day there. We would each be allotted a task. There were hundreds of chickens to be fed and watered, eggs to be gathered, and the pigs to care for. I loved helping to make the pig swill and watching the little piglets run about, squealing for their meal while mother pig grunted and snuffled, fussily rounding them up.

Auntie Margaret, surrounded by cousins Hilda, Ethel and children.

Through the summer there was fruit to be gathered from the orchard, hazelnuts to be picked from the hedges surrounding the fields of wheat, and peas and beans from the garden to be picked. Uncle Charles owned two beautiful shire horses to pull the plough, rake and harrow, each in season. He also kept a few cows, which I tended to avoid because of their unpredictable behaviour. My favourite occupation was feeding the pigs and the chickens and baby chicks. The chickens roamed free. There were hundreds of them and all sorts of varieties, including Rhode Island Reds, and White Leghorns, beautiful birds, the most colourful of all being the three or four cockerels, who proudly strutted around, showing off their brilliant, red, orange, yellow and russet plumage.

Mother (Nellie Hill), Arthur, Winnie, Cousin Hilda Hilda's son, Peggy (Hilda's daughter) and Hilda's sons visiting Potten End farm in 1933.

Some cousins, from Bletchley, also came to stay at the farm during the school holidays. The farmhouse was very large and well appointed, with hot and cold water available, and we were able take a bath whenever needed - a great luxury. Auntie Margaret spent her days in the kitchen making delicious meals for us all. On most days at least ten of us sat down for a wonderful lunch together. Afterwards, we 'youngsters' helped wash the dishes.

At the end of the day we children would sit outside, opposite the farmhouse, where a warren of rabbits would leave their burrows at sunset and come to feed in the grassy field. Keeping absolutely still and quiet, we would watch them for half-an-hour or so, then Arthur and I would stroll back to Granny's cottage, tired, contented and ready for bed. Granny Hill and family were a great support for Mother during those years.

Winnie and Cousin Peggy
on Uncle Charles' farm
in 1933.

(In the late 1980s Frank and I visited Potten End for an afternoon. Granny Hill's cottage was still there, although tiles had replaced the thatched roof. The Baptist Chapel also remained, but Uncle Charles' Farm had disappeared to become a building estate).

At Granny and Grandpa Edwards' house in Bedford we also spent some happy leisure hours. The house was situated not far from the main line railway station. The River Ouse runs right through Bedford and within the town its banks are lined with paved walks and flower beds and as it leaves the built up area these give way to open fields and pastures. We were lucky enough to live within a ten-minute walk of the more rural portion, and one of our favourite outings was to stroll along the river into 'Honey Hills'. Once there we were free to play, walk through the fields, catch a few small fish from the river, look for frogs, insects, have a picnic and sunbathe.

During these leisurely days Arthur was always with me, as he was very serious about his responsibility for his 'little sister'. We had many escapades and before leaving my childhood memories behind I will mention one or two significant episodes.

I must have been about ten years old, and Arthur thirteen. We were in Honey Hills, walking across a field full of cows when Arthur noticed a huge bull (probably not that huge but it appeared so to me at the time). 'Don't worry,' Arthur whispered. 'You're not wearing anything red. Just keep on walking steadily and he won't notice you. Keep looking at me instead.' I walked on as instructed but could not help stealing a quick, furtive glance across at the bull. 'He's looking at us Arthur,' I whispered, clutching his hand for reassurance. 'Don't worry,' he replied, but the very next moment we were aware of movement and noise, the bull's head was down and he was charging across the field straight for us.

I think I literally froze on the spot. Arthur grabbed me by the hand. 'Run, run, run,' he cried. We pelted towards the boundary fence and with one terrifying bound leapt over the fence and lay on the grass gasping for breath, with pounding hearts and trembling limbs. We looked up to see the bull standing just feet away on the other side of the fence. With a huge outlet of steamy breath, and a frustrated r-o-a-r he tossed his head, turned and walked away. We stayed where we were for quite a while, recovering from the shock, before creeping away. As far as I can remember that was the only time I ever jumped over a fence in one bound. This episode accounts for my lifelong fear of cows.

On another occasion when I was eight years old, once again in 'Honey Hills', the two of us were walking through the fields on a beautiful, hot, summer day when a thunderstorm blew up. Thunder was rolling around in the distance, dark clouds appeared in the sky, huge raindrops began to fall and we dashed for shelter under the solitary, huge, oak tree which stood in the middle of the field. The storm rapidly grew in strength, the world became filled with wind and noise, vivid lightning flashed across the sky, and then rain began to fall in torrents. Suddenly, Arthur grabbed my hand and hauled me from under the tree and out across the meadow into the open ground, shouting as we ran, 'Come on, run as fast as you can, we must get away from this tree.' 'Why?' I asked. 'It's so wet and cold in the rain. Mother will be angry if my dress gets wet and dirty.' 'I know,' he replied, 'but that's better than being struck by lightning.' Down we went, flat on our faces, into the wet grass, the storm raged around us, the earth shook, then came a mighty flash of lightning which struck the tree under which we had been sheltering and virtually split it apart. It was an absolutely awesome moment. We lay there in the grass aghast, mouths open, unable to speak for a few minutes. I looked at my clever brother in wonder. 'However did you know that tree would be struck?' He replied, 'Well, actually, I was not all that clever because I knew it was dangerous to shelter under a tree during a thunderstorm. Thank goodness I remembered in time.'

Near Honey Fields was a huge field called 'The Slipe'. A row of swings, a seesaw and small roundabout stood in a corner of the field, and alongside ran a stretch of the River Ouse, where it was deemed to be safe for swimming. The Town Council provided a changing room, which was opened during the summer months, with an attendant always on duty to keep an eye on the swimmers. One day, I went swimming there with a group of friends. Arthur was not with us. I must have been about fourteen by then. After the swim we lazed about for a while in the newly mown meadow grass. As we gathered our belongings together before returning home, I realised that my precious wristwatch, purchased from Marks and Spencer's for the princely sum of two shillings and sixpence, was missing. We searched high and low amongst the hay, virtually searching for 'a needle in a hay stack', but to no avail.

The following year, when walking past the bathing hut with Mother, we decided to search just once more for the watch. Mother thought it couldn't possibly have survived the winter cold and snow, however, imagine my delight when, after scrabbling amongst the grass stalks with a twig, we caught sight of something shiny. I could hardly believe my eyes, but there was my watch, looking a little worse for wear but still intact. The casing was not rusty, although the wrist strap looked forlorn. After I turned the winder the watch immediately began to tick. What an advertisement for Marks and Spencer's 'quality for money'! I bought a new wrist strap and continued wearing the watch for many years.

A year or two later I was there again with a group of about ten friends swimming in the river without supervision. I can only suppose we did so thinking that we were adult enough to avoid danger. It was a beautiful warm, sunny day and all went well until we got out of the water. It was then that we became aware that one of the girls was missing from the group. The boys dived into the water again and began to search along the edge of the weedy section, to no avail. We called out, searched again, still no success. Sadly, in the end we had to assume that our missing friend had strayed into the weedy area and become entangled. It was a heart-breaking time, we all learnt a salutary lesson and now you can understand why I was never very enthusiastic about entering the water. In fact after this I did not swim again.

From this period of my life another picture will always remain imprinted in my mind. It is a typical rural scene from the past. Every Sunday morning dressed in their best clothes, Granny Hill, Uncle Charles and Auntie Margaret, all loyal members of the Baptist Chapel, attended morning service. If you were there you would have seen, walking side by side, Uncle Charles, dressed in fawn coloured breeches, highly polished brown leather gaiters, black jacket, hat and walking stick, and Auntie Margaret, in her best gown and wide brimmed straw hat, solemnly leading a crocodile, which included four or five of our cousins together with their parents, along the road from the farm towards Chapel. When the crocodile reached Granny Hill's cottage she joined Uncle Charles at the head of the crocodile, and Arthur and I tagged on at the tail end, along with our cousins. In this formation we all filed through the Chapel door and took our seats. This was the routine every Sunday when we stayed with Granny Hill.

Uncle Charles often conducted the service and I recall one time vividly, (such moments do tend to stick in the mind). Uncle was announcing a hymn in full voice. 'We will now sing hymn number h'eight hundred and h'eighty h'eight,' he said. You can imagine the reaction of us seven children, sitting together in the same row. Uncle Charles was such a loving, caring man and his diction and grammar were always excellent. Quite why he had this difficulty with the number eight on that particular morning I do not know. You might get the impression that I was always giggling. Far from it, really on my own I was rather quiet and serious.

1935 - 1938

On leaving school in 1935 my ambition was to become a nurse and then offer myself for service with the Moravian Church, either in Africa or Labrador. Knowing there was a waiting list for entry to the Nurses' Training School I immediately applied to Bedford County Hospital, and, after passing their entrance requirements, my name was placed on the register to commence training in September 1937. Immediately after this I set about finding a fulltime paid job. Thus began two years of working in the office of a local Timber Merchant.

The 'Enquiries' office, situated next to the huge Saw Mill, was my domain. There I would perch on a high stool, sitting very straight backed because by then I, like my friends, was wearing a whalebone corset, deemed by our parents to be a vital item of clothing for maintaining good posture. Actually, the bones dug into our ribs and were so painful that most of us cut small slits into the material and slid the bones out - the corsets were still quite supportive without them. There I sat, behind a long, glass fronted, sloping desk, and dealt with all enquiries, from the mill workers with cut fingers to travelling salesmen. In one corner of the office was a letterpress, this being the only means of copying letters apart from using carbon paper for typewritten work. The Works Manager and two clerks shared a larger office room next door, and beyond this were two further rooms, one occupied by Mr. Martin, owner of the mill, and the other by his Personal Secretary.

This turned out to be an interesting experience. One of my tasks was to accompany Mr. Martin whenever he made an inspection round of the acres of seasoning sheds. On these occasions he would hand me a clipboard, to which lists were attached, giving details on the country of origin, type of timber, its age, and notes showing how long the sawn timber had been lying in the stacking shed. This taught me a lot about timber, the running of a sawmill, the stacking and seasoning of timber and the routine of a busy office.

Regularly each Friday morning, I would walk alone, across the town to the Bank, to collect and carry back to the Mill sufficient cash for the wages of the entire workforce, about fifty in all, from the Manager down to the humblest sweeper in the sawmill.

Another task allotted to me was the typing of individual specifications for the making of greenhouses, wooden stables for horses, chicken coops and garden sheds. These were sent out to prospective customers, together with a further typed letter. Since the wording of the letters was fairly standard, typing them individually helped to increase my typing speed.

My office was lit by one electric light, which hung from the ceiling, just above my head. One day the light flex broke and the bulb, together with its glass shade, fell to the ground, hitting my head on its way down, and creating the most terrific noise in the process. The Works Manager and two clerks rushed from their room to find me with a cut on my head, the floor covered with shattered glass and an exposed electric wire dangling from the ceiling. Everyone was most attentive, out came the First Aid box, always kept ready in case anyone in the sawmill needed attention, and I went home that evening with a white patch stuck to the cut on my head.

It was during this period that I attended night school to study book keeping and shorthand typing, with the idea that these skills might come in useful in the future. And they did, especially when working in China and later in India.

Time had brought about a number of changes within the household. Auntie Gladys and Uncle George both married and set up their own houses. Then, in the autumn of 1936 Granny Edwards became ill with pneumonia and passed away. I remember the occasion very clearly, because at the same time Mother was extremely ill with a quinsy and a very high temperature, so caring for both of them was up to me. Granny was delirious and kept getting out of bed and wandering around her bedroom. I was frantic with worry because the gas fire in her room was alight and I feared that her flowing nightdress might brush against the fire and catch alight. Poor old Grandpa just sat in his chair downstairs and left me to make all arrangements for the death certificate, undertakers and funeral.

I do not quite know why, but despite the fact that three of mother's brothers and Aunty Gladys were all living in Bedford, nobody came to help, although all turned up for the funeral and food afterwards. One Uncle even took me aside after the funeral and said. 'You'd better take good care of your Mother or she'll be next to go.'

We recovered from this trauma, and Grandpa decided that he would go and take up residence with Auntie Gladys. Arthur, in the meantime, had offered himself to the Moravian Church for theological training. He received a grant and went to Theological College in Manchester for three years. He was ordained into the Ministry in 1940, married in 1941, and a year later was sent to work overseas in the West Indies. Initially, he was stationed in Tobago and later moved to British Guyana. Usually missionaries were commissioned to serve for five years abroad, followed by one year of 'furlough' in England, but because of the Second World War restrictions, Arthur did not return home until 1948/49. Consequently, it was many years before we met again.

As a result of these changes Mother and I were alone in the old family house, until September 1937, when I started upon my nursing career and left home to take up residence in the Nurses' Home. Our living quarters were quite comfortable and we took meals in the hospital dining room. During the first three months of Preliminary Training most of our time was spent studying anatomy, hygiene, bandaging and other related subjects.

Only after successfully completing the course were we allowed on the wards. Working hours were long compared to today's standards and we received five shillings a month pocket money with free board and lodging. Uniforms were provided, comprising three white aprons, four white, starched caps, and two dresses with a finished skirt length of 'no more than eight inches above the floor'. To allow for material shrinkage when washed, two large tucks would always be stitched all around the bottom of a new skirt, just above the hem. Theoretically, these tucks were meant to be taken out after the first few washes but, being young students, we tried to get away with ignoring this.

Once on the wards I was in my element, walking tall and talking to the patients while making beds, dusting lockers, emptying bedpans and tidying beds ready for Matron's round. There were twenty beds in each ward. One morning while on duty on the Men's Ward, I was dusting a bedside locker with my head facing the wall, when out of nowhere a loud voice called, 'Nurse, stand up this minute. You are showing the backs of your knees. Let that hem down at once.' Blushing crimson, I meekly replied, 'Yes, Matron'. Needless to say, on that ward every time I bent over, one or other of the men could be heard saying, 'For shame nurse, you are showing the backs of your knees.' Incidents like this gave so much fun. I did unstitch one tuck as a token gesture.

Sadly, my dream of a nursing career did not materialize, because soon after starting work on the wards I developed an infected fingernail that was extremely slow to heal. As a result, I was dismissed as 'unsuitable for the nursing profession because too susceptible to infection'. This was absolutely devastating for me. All my hopes for the future were dashed, and it became a very low period of my life.

Nevertheless, it was vital that I earn my daily bread, and to that end I hastily set about finding a job, eventually obtaining a post as Secretary to the Manager of the local 'Roses Fashion Store', one of a chain of six shops situated in various towns throughout the southern part of the country.

This turned out to be an enjoyable post because, in addition to my secretarial work, the proprietor of the business often called upon me to act as a 'model' when new stock arrived in the stockroom. The Bedford shop catered for the more affluent type of clientele and the garments were of excellent quality, including beautiful, long, fur coats and gorgeous evening gowns.

One of the perks of working at
Roses Fashion Store
was that I could purchase clothes at cost price.
I became a very smartly dressed young lady
during those years.

Maybe I have made my young adult life sound altogether too serious, but this was not so. Within St. Peter's Moravian Church fellowship I had grown up with a group of about thirty young people. Over the years our activities included serious discussions regarding Christianity and how it applied to our way of life, but we also taught in Sunday School, sang in the choir and arranged social meetings and amateur concerts.

The Christian Faith was a source of great hope and strength to those, who like my mother, suffered personal loss and great hardship as a result of the First World War. As a young child I accepted the stories about Jesus and angels 'above the bright blue sky' in the same way as I believed for a while in Father Christmas. As I became older and read the Gospels and Acts of the Apostles, I thought more deeply about the teachings of Christ, my faith grew and I was confirmed as a member of the

Moravian Church. The centre of our belief was to serve and love one another, all being equal in the sight of God. This was the mainstay of my personal faith from which sprang my longing to work abroad amongst the poor and needy. In a truly amazing way you will see how, as my life unfolded, so many of my experiences along the way were to prove ideal for the situations in which I later found myself. It was also this strong belief on which we all depended in order to make sense of the cruel, senseless years of World War One and its aftermath.

Mother in the garden of my grandparents' house in Bedford. She enjoyed knitting and made garments for all the family well into her nineties.

During the summer we would spend leisure time punting on the river or cycling around the countryside generally enjoying ourselves.

Once I became independent financially it was possible for me to venture into a social world quite separate from the church. After an audition, I became a member of the Bedford Choral Society, as well as the Operatic Society.

At about this time, I was also saving a small amount of money each week from my wages, and one day I noticed an advertisement in the daily paper.

> Upright Broadwood Piano only seventeen guineas.
> Payment over twelve, monthly instalments.
> Place your order now.
> Selfridges, London.

Buying anything by hire purchase took great courage, as we had been brought up to 'NEVER buy anything unless you have the money with which to pay for it'. After much soul searching, I plucked up courage and placed an order. The piano duly arrived and was paid for within twelve months. Of course, when the piano was actually standing in the house I realised that ten years had passed since I had touched one. Lessons, being too costly, were out of the question. A kind friend advised me to sight read every hymn in the hymnbook. 'In this way,' he said, I 'would learn by recognising the tune and knowing if I made a mistake, and I would gain knowledge of playing using almost every scale'.

This proved to be excellent advice, and I found that I had retained my sight reading skill, largely, I feel sure, because my erstwhile, very strict, piano teacher had always rapped my knuckles really hard with a ruler if ever, when playing, I dared to look at my fingers instead of the reading the music before my eyes. I practiced diligently and virtually became self-taught.

Later our organist taught me to play the lovely, three manual, pipe organ in St. Peter's Moravian Church. I could not have guessed it at the time, but all of this experience was to prove very useful in China and later in India.

1939 - 1947

It was during the last week of August 1939 that I travelled, by train via London, to spend a week with my Great Auntie Lucy (sister to Granny Edwards) at her home in Dartford, Kent.

Winnie, in holiday spirit
with Great Auntie Lucy
summer 1927.

Although Auntie's hat looks as if it was levitating, I think it was just propped on a stick.

We dearly loved Aunt Lucy, and throughout my childhood years she always spent Christmas with us. Her bright, bubbly personality was very contagious. She was profoundly deaf and when young, Arthur and I were always fascinated by the enormous trumpet through which we had to shout in order to communicate with her. This trumpet was about eighteen inches long with a tiny opening at the top, which fitted into Auntie's ear, and a wide opening at the bottom through which we shouted. No matter whether she understood our conversation or not, Auntie would always laugh. Auntie Lucy owned a large house and made a living by 'taking in' lodgers, seven young businessmen, catering for their every need. At the time of my visit news was coming through the radio about the possibility of war with Germany, but, on the whole, for the average citizen, life was going along as usual. Rumours of war and disagreements in Europe were forever being reported through the media, but we all hoped that war could be avoided.

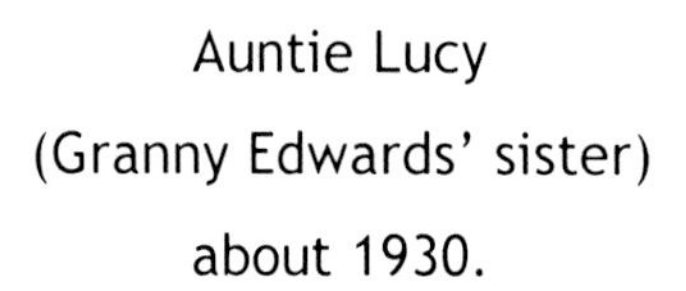

Auntie Lucy
(Granny Edwards' sister)
about 1930.

Little did I realise that Sunday 3rd September 1939, would become a very significant day. On that very day I accompanied Auntie Lucy to Church for the morning service and halfway through the sermon we heard the sound of an aircraft engine droning overhead. Scarcely had this sound faded away, when there came the loud, tummy churning, wail of an air raid siren. For an instant everyone in the congregation seemed stunned, then, the Minister closed the service, solemnly announcing that War must have been declared and 'since there was a plane flying around and we were near the East coast, we should all return home immediately and take cover'.

Poor Auntie, she was utterly confused. I tried to encourage her to walk home quickly and she became very distressed when an angry, red-faced, Air Raid Warden rushed up to us shouting, 'Get indoors quickly can't y're. What on earth do y're think y're doing walking around outside with an air raid on?' It was pandemonium. Auntie had no inkling that War might be declared. With her degree of deafness, listening to the radio was out of the question, and she was so busy looking after her 'young men' that she rarely looked at a newspaper. Thankfully, we eventually reached home, and shortly afterwards the 'All Clear' sounded. It was then that I discovered Auntie had no blackout curtains ready to be hung at the windows. We had been advised, through the media, to prepare such curtains in case of need. In the event of an air raid, streetlights were to be extinguished and all private houses and shops must be blacked out. Even car headlights were to be dimmed. I rushed out, purchased lots of black material and set about making curtains for the twenty or so windows in the house. Auntie's lodgers were a great help hanging the curtains. That most important task accomplished, my holiday time was over and I returned home to Bedford.

After the first period of nervous apprehension we began to witness the departure of thousands of young men to fight, some voluntarily, others being 'called up' for military service. I often wonder what must have passed through the minds of those who had lost family members as a result of the First World War only twenty or so years earlier. They must have felt so sad seeing it happening all over again.

As for myself, I continued working in Roses Fashion Centre. I did not volunteer for military service because Mother was not keen on being left alone. During the initial days of the War each street organised its own Air Raid Programme.

Residents talked amongst themselves regarding the procedure to be adopted in the event of an Air Raid. I became an Air Raid Warden. This meant being on call three nights each week. A small wooden shed for our use was set up, furnished with a couple of chairs, a primus stove, tea making equipment and some biscuits. In addition, there was a first aid box. Also on hand were buckets of water and stirrup pumps with which we hoped to extinguish a fire should a passing enemy aircraft drop some incendiary bombs.

Being 'on call' meant that in the event of the air raid siren being sounded we would patrol up and down the street, making sure there were no lights showing and that people took cover as much as possible. From time to time we would return to the hut for a cup of tea and a 'fag'. This was when I tasted my first cigarette.

Bedford escaped air raids, although night after night we could see the fires of London reflected in the night sky. Eventually, when Coventry was being attacked relentlessly every night, we would hear the distinctive drone of the German bombers as they flew over Bedford on their way to do their work. A few hours later we would hear the planes returning from a raid, and know that their fatal work had been accomplished by the changed tone of the engines. The people of Coventry were in our minds all through the night.

As I have said, Bedford itself was not really troubled by direct air raids and life went on as usual for almost two years after War had been declared. However, during this time, London and the south east of the country were being battered. Initially, in 1939, hundreds of children had been evacuated out of London. Many drifted back home because they missed home and their families felt a need to be together facing the dangers.

Early in 1941 I received my 'call-up' and opted for local 'war work' so that I would be at hand for Mother. I was directed to work in the Bedford County Hospital for the duration.

Winnie and two friends
at Bedford County Hospital
in 1945.

My duties were, 'To be responsible for the welfare of all Service personnel admitted to the hospital'. This meant keeping an eye on their family circumstances as well as their health, doling out the weekly ration of cigarettes and sweets, and communicating with their family members. A good number of Army and Air Force men were admitted, some with terrific injuries caused by accidents during manoeuvres, but I found it rather a tedious job.

Looking back there were times of challenge. One poor chap had been trapped under a tank when it toppled over into a pond. The massive injuries he sustained to his legs meant that both were amputated. The great tragedy was that in civilian life he was a coalman and the sole wage earner in the family. My task was to keep in touch with his family and try to help them through the trauma. Another incident was an air crash, which happened on Christmas Eve, when all the crew were killed. Their bodies were delivered to the hospital mortuary. I had to retrieve all their personal papers and possessions, inform the families and deal with the whole situation, made much more tragic by the fact that it was over the Christmas period.

Apart from these isolated incidents my duties were very light. Perhaps, the greatest advantage was that I could continue living at home to keep Mother company. As I mentioned earlier, Arthur was away in the West Indies throughout the War.

I paid a visit to Auntie Lucy shortly after beginning this posting because the air raids in and around London had been very severe and we were worried for her safety. Auntie was coping very well indeed, although she did not have as many lodgers as before. When I reached St. Pancras railway station during my return journey to Bedford I found it absolutely packed with rows and rows of children, standing forlornly, dressed in school uniform, gas mask and name tag hanging from their necks, each carrying a small suitcase or box. The Government had suddenly decided that the bombing in London was again so severe that the children must be sent away to the countryside.

Harassed ladies carrying clip boards bustled about amongst the children, trying to sort out who was to go where. The station was so crowded that it was difficult to find out what was really going on. Worried about reporting for duty in Bedford, I sought the aid of a porter who managed to squeeze me into a carriage along with a host of anxious, young children, who had been marshalled into the train. An official, who would take them to their ultimate destination, escorted each group of children. Watching the film, 'Goodnight, Mr. Tom', on the television recently, this whole scene was brought vividly back to mind.

Prior to 1947, hospitals such as Bedford County received their financial support from voluntary contributions. In addition, local firms deducted one penny per week from all their workers and the money raised was given to the hospital to cover cost of treatment as required. Money was also raised through an Annual Sale during the summer. All the Consultants gave their professional services free to the Hospital. It was they who came to me one day and asked whether I would assist them with their outpatient correspondence. I was only too glad to have something challenging to do. I purchased a medical dictionary and became part-time secretary to eight Honorary Consultants in different specialties, picking up a great deal of information about different diseases and injuries as I went along. I am not sure but I like to think that I was the first Medical Secretary in the UK.

Later my duties widened and I was asked to assist in the Orthopaedic Clinic, removing plasters and escorting patients to and from the X-Ray department. During the War it was very difficult to recruit workers and hospital funds were extremely short, so we all willingly gave extra services freely.

When the Second World War came to an end in 1945, my wartime posting also ended. But it was no problem as the Hospital Board appointed me as Medical Secretary, Matron's Secretary and Wages Clerk, and gave me my own office in the Administration Block next to Matron's Office and the Resident Housemen's Quarters.

At the time it was obligatory for a newly qualified doctor to undertake four, six-monthly hospital appointments, each in a different specialty (Surgery, Medicine, General Practice and so on), before going for further training. There was a very friendly atmosphere amongst the staff and it was natural for me to speak to the new housemen when they arrived.

One doctor I especially remember was Dr. Adler. He had arrived at Bedford County during the war years, a Jewish refugee from Nazi Germany and had been on the staff for three of four years. We were great friends and he always made the new young doctors feel at home when they first arrived. He did not really want to talk about his earlier life and we ordinary citizens did not receive much news about what was taking place in Germany during the years leading up to and during the Second World War. It was only later, through films and books, that we learnt the full story of the great sufferings of the Jewish people.

Frank appeared on the scene during the latter half of 1946, a young, shy, newly qualified doctor, for his six months surgical appointment. The first words he ever spoke to me were, 'Please, Miss Hill, could you tell me where the nearest Post Office is?' Later, when chatting with Dr. Adler I learnt that Frank was planning to go abroad for the Methodist Missionary Society as soon as he had passed the FRCS examination. I can still picture Dr. Adler saying, 'There you are Miss Hill, just the very man for you, with your interest in work overseas.' 'Oh no,' I said, 'don't you dare try any match making stunt.' I must admit that on learning of Frank's plans to work abroad for the Church my curiosity was aroused, but because of Dr. Adler's remarks, I was hesitant to speak to Frank, and he appeared to be very shy and wary of me. Little did I know then that Dr. Adler had been admonishing him to the effect that I would make him an excellent wife because we both held the same aspirations.

It so happened that the Rev Driver and his doctor wife, home from Leh in Tibet on furlough, were planning to give a lantern lecture at St. Peter's Moravian Church, about their work. I invited Frank to the lecture and he came. The Drivers were anxious to take a helper back to Leh with them and I tentatively offered to go, subject to approval from Mission House and health checks. I thought this would be my great opportunity to work abroad helping those less fortunate than me and Tibet seemed to be so remote and challenging.

Food was still rationed. Fresh fruit, in particular, was difficult to obtain and from time to time I would purchase a special treat for the Housemen. Hospital food for them was good but basic, and their salary really low. Hence, on one occasion in the latter months of 1946, Frank became the recipient of a gorgeous red apple, my first gift to him. This was the beginning of the following saga, and it was to prove Dr. Adler correct in his assumption that we were meant for each other.

Frank's appointment at Bedford County Hospital came to an end and he went to work in the Postgraduate School at Hammersmith for six months, prior to taking the FRCS examination. During that time we corresponded regularly and Frank visited me at home for a couple of weekends. We often talked about the future but everything was on hold until after the outcome of the all-important examination.

One morning late in November 1947 the telephone in Matron's office rang. I picked it up and an excited voice cried, 'I've passed. I've passed.' There was great excitement and rejoicing. Frank had now become a fully qualified Fellow of the Royal College of Surgeons, a successful end to his years of dedication and hard work. On the strength of this momentous event Frank and I became engaged.

Frank took me to Bath for a weekend and we stayed with his parents in 'Steep Holm', Bathampton. This was my first experience of spending time in the home of anyone other than family and I felt a little in awe of Frank's father. His mother was a very sweet, gentle lady. His father questioned me closely, asking whether I felt I was a suitable person to make Frank a good wife.

Winnie Hill
and Frank Tovey.
Our engagement photo,
November 1947.

Frank's Auntie Irene lived in a bungalow very near Steep Holm. Surrounding the bungalow was a huge garden including an orchard, her great pride and joy and our delight. We also visited Auntie May, who lived with her Japanese Spaniel dogs (she had about ten dogs at the time) in the old family home half way up Lansdown Road. The house was very large, with five storeys including the basement and attic, and it was elegantly furnished in comparison to my humble home in Bedford.

Having visited Bath, I realised that Frank's family circumstances were, and always had been, vastly different from mine. Frank had received a private school education, immediately followed by years as a medical student, always remaining entirely dependent upon his parents until he took his first House Surgeon appointment, and only then becoming a wage earner. His brother John was a medical student, and his father and Auntie Irene were qualified opticians.

Frank's grandfather, Frank Ivor Tovey, was descended from a family of watch and clock makers. He had qualified as an optician and set up the business in New Bond Street, Bath. It was here that Frank's father, Ernest Tovey worked. Ernest trained as an optician when courting Nellie and had to change his name from Short to Tovey by deed poll when he married her, the eldest of the three Tovey daughters.

Frank's auntie, Irene Tovey, also worked at the shop in Bath. She was the middle sister to Nellie and May and the first woman to qualify as an optician in England, for which she was awarded the Freedom of London.

During the weekend I spent a fascinating afternoon in the shop. I met all the staff members and then was taken upstairs into the workshop where spectacles were prepared for individual customers. At that time, 1947, spectacle lenses were made of glass and arrived in squares. First of all the lens had to be centred. If they were cylindrical the axis was marked with a blue pencil, then the lenses were cut, using a template, and bevelled to fit the spectacle frame. If bifocal correction was required, this was added as a segment, which was stuck onto the lower part of the lens. It needed great skill and care to obtain a good result. I found it fascinating.

Frank, of course, knew all about my background and had visited our house frequently, but I was slightly worried about what his family expected of me because of my working class background. Quietly, I was overwhelmed. Despite the fact that in view of our family circumstances I had successfully worked my way through to obtain a responsible post with a good salary, I did wonder whether Frank's father would be happy to accept me as a suitable partner for his son.

The weekend passed very quickly. I returned to Bedford and work, whilst Frank immediately reported to Dr. Ralph Bolton, Medical Secretary of the Methodist Missionary Society, that he was available for service overseas.

The next day a message came back asking whether he could be ready to sail to China within two weeks. His reply was, 'Yes, providing he could be married and travel to China with his new wife'. The Mission Board answered, 'according to the rules, you can only be married after you have completed two years' service in China'. Frank replied that he was not willing to go under such terms. There was a tense wait, but on the next day a telephone message came asking if we could get married and be ready to sail in two weeks' time.

On hearing this, Matron Shand's first reaction was that it was impossible because I needed to give four weeks notice before leaving my employment. Amazingly, when it was put to the Hospital Board they granted permission for me to leave within a few days.

Frank and I received great encouragement and support from the whole medical and nursing staff. They, like us, were full of excitement about the whole enterprise. China was an exotic and mysterious place that had been relatively cut off from the outside world for years.

The other important thing I had to do was, of course, to notify the Moravian Church Board that I would not be able to accompany the Rev and Mrs Driver when they returned to Tibet. They were very gracious about the situation and sent their sincere best wishes.

I felt sad at leaving Mother, as Arthur was still abroad and she would be alone at home. Whatever she might have felt, she was most supportive of all our plans. Shortly after we left England, she was appointed as a House Mistress in Ockbrook Girls' School on a Moravian Settlement near Derby. She moved to live there and spent all the years we were abroad in Ockbrook, living at first in the school, and later in a flat within the Settlement, where she was extremely happy.

In a whirl of activity Frank and I entered into the formidable task of arranging to be married by Special Licence and undergoing all the medical checks and inoculations required for entry into China. We had very little knowledge about China itself and knew nothing about the activities of the Methodist Church out there. Mission House advised us to read a couple of books written by Methodist Missionaries who had worked in the Hankow and Yunnan areas.

We were due to sail from Glasgow on the 'TSS Empire Brent'. Mercifully, the sailing date was postponed by a week, which gave us three weeks in which to prepare.

Mission House supplied us with a long list of the items that they considered essential to take: clothing, bedding, cooking utensils, cutlery and sufficient toiletries, shoelaces, shoe polish, toothpaste and other sundries, enough to last for five years. We were directed to Alinson's exporters, specialists in equipping people to go abroad. They supplied us with a list of goods and we just ticked off items and quantities. They then proceeded to pack, crate and forward the boxes directly to the ship. Almost the whole consignment did not see the light of day until we unpacked it in Chaotung nine months later.

Some things were still rationed and in order to obtain bedding we needed to apply for special coupons. These were granted. One of the inoculations required was for yellow fever, which entailed a special visit to the Tropical Diseases Hospital in London. The allowance of bedding for newly weds was two double size utility blankets, three double sheets and four pillow cases. The blankets were not available in Bedford, so we decided to buy these from Gamages whilst in London for the inoculations.

Unfortunately, even in Gamages, the blankets were not available in the shop itself. Because of the urgency of our situation, the shop assistant escorted us down into the depths of their warehouse for them. We must have looked absolutely crazy, laden with all this bedding, struggling through the Underground across London to Alinson's where we delivered our burden for packing into the crates to be sent to China. We made it in time, and the blankets travelled to China and back with us, later to be taken to India. One was used in the early 1960s as part of the costume for Jenny, John and David who dressed as a dhobi and his donkey on the P&O liner trip from India to England on furlough. The same blankets were still in regular use twenty-five years after their journey on the Underground.

The frantic activity of those three weeks was relentless. I had to undergo a complete medical check-up, which, because I was found to be extremely anaemic, included a sternal puncture to extract some bone marrow. This procedure was excruciatingly painful. It was also considered necessary for Frank's lower wisdom teeth to be removed and both were pulled out in one session under local anaesthetic - a painful time for him also.

As for the wedding, our clothing coupons were all used up, so I borrowed a wedding dress from my cousin Marjorie. I had to turn the hem up by about four inches, but otherwise the dress was a good fit. We were married by Special Licence in the St. Peter's Moravian Church, Bedford on Friday, December 11th 1947.

From left to right, my mother, Nellie Hill, Frank's brother, John, Frank, me, Connie Humberstone, and Frank's mother and father, Nellie and Ernest Tovey.

Because of food rationing we were limited to twenty-four guests at the reception. Even though it was a very cold, wintry day, with snow still lying on the ground, lots of friends attended the service and gave us a great send off. There was no time for an immediate honeymoon as we would be spending six weeks on the sea, so we went to Bath for the weekend. On the following Tuesday a Valedictory Service was held at Walcot Street Methodist Church in Bath attended by a huge crowd of Frank's family and friends.

On the 16th December, Wednesday afternoon, we started the long train journey to Glasgow. The train was unheated and without sleeping facilities. We travelled through the night, wearing our overcoats, woolly hats and gloves, and trying to sleep, huddled together for warmth. At about 11a.m. on Thursday morning, the train shunted onto the Glasgow quayside alongside the 'Empire Brent'. Fortunately, Alinson's consignment of goods was already stowed away on the ship and all we had to do was hand over our personal baggage for loading, show our passports and surrender our Ration Books. This felt very odd. We had carried them around for so many years that we felt bereft without them. When all was done we were free to board the ship.

Surrounded by dozens of fellow travellers, I climbed up the gangway and took my first ever steps on board a ship. Frank, having lived in Bristol during his student days, had been on board a ship before and he enjoyed showing me the way around. I wanted to explore every nook and cranny.

What an amazing feeling it was! I am sure our eyes must have been sparkling with joy, at last we were setting off on our voyage of discovery and adventure, both in our lives together and in a country almost unknown to us. We looked around at our fellow passengers, as I am sure they looked upon us, wondering what had caused them all to make this exciting journey. Here we were on Thursday, 17th December 1947, boarding a ship, which would carry us across the oceans to a far off land -

CHINA.

The Sea Voyage - December 17th 1947 to January 23rd 1948

Frank and I arrived at the docks after most of the other passengers, owing to the fact that our train was late reaching Glasgow. Once our boarding formalities were over we were quickly conducted onto the ship and to our respective cabins; women and children on the main deck in large cabins for sixteen persons, and men on the lower deck in similar sized cabins. All baths, showers and toilets were communal and serviced by seawater. Fresh water was only available through the hand washbasins.

We had arrived in Glasgow late in the morning after a long cold train journey and we were very hungry. What an event was that first lunch on board! We were still used to food rationing, but here we were, just one step off the shore, being offered a five course menu of soup, fish, meat, dessert, bread rolls, butter, sugar and a variety of beautiful fresh fruit such as we had not seen for years, all rounded off with a cup of delicious coffee and a wee chocolate mint. What a beginning to our honeymoon. The only sad thing was that after years of rationing none of us could do justice to such an abundance of food at one meal.

During the afternoon we returned to our cabins to unpack our personal belongings and generally settle in. Fortunately we were all travelling with a very light wardrobe, quantity being limited by clothes rationing, and there was no difficulty in fitting sixteen people into the confined space of the cabins. Once our suitcases were empty, the cabin boys whisked them away to be stored in the hold.

The ship was a converted transport vessel and looked enormous to us, although it was only 11,000 tons. We set sail during the night of 17/18th December, travelling down the Irish Sea, past Land's End and across the Bay of Biscay to Gibraltar. Frank and I quickly settled down to life afloat.

The TSS
(Twin Screw Ship)
'Empire Brent'

Before each meal the married men waited patiently in front of the Purser's Office for their wives, so that they could go together into the dining room. Throughout the voyage we sat at a table with Tom and Connie Richardson and Gertrude Hughes, who were fellow missionaries. Tom and Connie had already spent many years working in China, but Gertrude, a nurse, was going for the first time. We did much together.

On Christmas Day we were in the Mediterranean Sea and during the evening we celebrated with a little party on deck when we cut the top tier of our wedding cake, in place of a Christmas cake.

The ship stopped at Port Said and Port Suez. It was very hot indeed crossing the Red Sea and, with the ventilation on board being extremely poor, many passengers slept on deck. We tried it once, only to be hosed down when the decks were washed very early in the morning.

Further ports of call during our journey were Bombay, Penang and Singapore.

From here onward you will find most of our story told through extracts from letters written by myself and Frank at the time. Most of the letters that were kept were to Frank's parents, Nellie and Ernest Tovey, with some to Frank's Aunt Irene and a few to his brother John. Unless otherwise noted the letters are to Frank's parents.

Christmas Day 1947 - letter written over several days on 'TSS Empire Brent' and posted in Port Said on 28th December.

Frank:-

It is a Christmas Day such as one never dreams of seeing at home. The sun is shining brilliantly and the sea is quite smooth and calm, and such a deep blue. Winnie and I are sitting out in the sun in summer attire and trying to imagine what you are all doing at home. Early this afternoon we passed Malta and were really quite surprised to find it is not such a very small island after all.

Winnie:-

Frank has just gone off to find a cup of tea so I thought I would insert a paragraph. Today has been quite like Christmas here. At 6a.m. some brave people arose and went round singing carols. I was up at 6 o'clock and joined Frank on deck until 7 o'clock when we went to a Communion Service, then we had breakfast - just an ordinary breakfast as served aboard but a wonderful one - grapefruit, cornflakes, fish if wanted, fried egg and bacon, hot cakes and syrup to follow if tummy permitted, scones and toast and marmalade. It isn't fair on you for us to enlarge upon the wonderful meals we are having. They are quite unbelievable. After breakfast, we went to the ship's Christmas service. The Captain has asked one of the senior missionaries on board to be responsible for all the ship's services. It was very simple service and we all felt very much at one with you having your own service in the chapel at Bathampton.

Frank:-

The children have all been so excited today, they had a wonderful time opening their presents early in the morning. At this moment they're enjoying a Christmas party to be followed by a lantern show.

We are having our Christmas Dinner tonight. The dining room is delightfully decorated and we are all dressing for the occasion. Winnie has hastily looked out her long frock as she realised that the others had prepared theirs. After dinner, we plan to have a special little party of our own when we are going to cut the wedding cake and play party games. Last night, the 'carol party' sang carols on deck and the crew gave a concert. At dinner, all the children (there are 200 on board) came around and sang carols as we ate.

December 27th 1947 - letter to Frank's brother John, from 'TSS Empire Brent'.

Frank:-

We have to post our letters on board ship this evening at 6 o'clock. Christmas Day ended very happily, we had a wonderful Christmas dinner and then went on the foredeck for a Christmas party of our own. We were just 10 in all. We cut the wedding cake (it was a super cake) and shared it out, also ate chocolate and drank ginger beer, then we played games until nearly midnight.

We should arrive in Port Said at 1a.m. tomorrow 28th December 1947 so should see something of the harbour. It is going to be very exciting going through the Suez Canal, it is a thing I have always longed to do.

Christmas Day 1947 - letter to Frank's parents, contd.

Frank:-

There are about 680 passengers on board - the full contingent is 984. About 60 are missionaries, a really large number. All are very friendly, and there is a grand comradeship throughout the boat. We Methodists number just five. There is Gertrude Hughes, a nurse, aged 27. The others are, Connie and Tom Richardson. Tom has been in China for 12 years, he teaches in a school near Hankow. They have three boys, aged 11 and 5 years and the youngest 6 months. Tom and Connie are good company. Each morning, Tom is giving us a short talk about China, which is proving very helpful.

The boat has made excellent progress - about 380 miles each day. The weather has been very warm - even in the Irish Sea we could sit on deck without overcoats - and the sea has been absolutely calm, except for yesterday, when there was a little swell which made the boat roll. Gibraltar we passed in the night on Monday. Since entering the Mediterranean we have had to put our watches on 30 minutes each night.

The crew are mostly Scottish, so they have made a good deal of New Year. On New Year's Day, we had a marvellous dinner, which came as quite a surprise to many of us.

Tom Richardson continues to give us tutorials in the morning and they are proving very helpful. Winnie is also learning some medicine from me and is a very able scholar. On Friday, we had a lecture on 'Chinese Philosophy' from a Chinese professor; we hope to have another one next week on 'Etiquette'.

Our circle of friends seems to grow and we are always finding interesting people. We have got to know the ship's Medical Officer and he has very kindly invited us to use his cabin. The ship should arrive in Port Said on Saturday. The only port at which we shall stay for more than a few hours is Bombay, we should arrive there on January the 4th and may stay for four days. If the weather holds good, January 21st is our day of arrival at Hong Kong.

We are quite comfortable on board although it is a little hard being separated. We are in sixteen berth cabins arranged in groups. Each group of cabins has a washroom and bathroom etc. We have to do our own laundry but otherwise are well looked after. Winnie is already looking much better and, judging by my trousers, I am getting quite a big tummy.

We have met Miss Gale, and I have met an Indian E.N.T. surgeon who was studying in London. The missionary group are holding daily meetings but they are of the rather overemotional type and Winnie and I feel it is better to use the time for reading and other study. Altogether it is proving a very restful and wonderful time and we are most thankful for it.

Although we were under the auspices of M.M.S. (Methodist Missionary Society), Frank and I were not intending to 'convert' people as such; our motivation was more to endeavour to show God's love as far as possible in the way we lived and treated those less fortunate than ourselves. Sometimes, we felt somewhat isolated from our fellow missionaries on the field because we had not spent time in Selly Oak, a College to which most MMS candidates were sent for a period of orientation before going to work overseas. Nevertheless, when we got to China we found so much work to do in the hospitals that there was no time to worry about this.

Prior to leaving England Frank purchased two books, 'Understanding China' and 'Let my people know' by Harold B. Rattenbury, a Methodist minister who spent many years working in China. In 'Understanding China', published in 1942, the Reverend Rattenbury begins with these words 'The China of 1942 is so different from the China of forty years ago as to be unbelievable if it were not true.' The same statement rings true in 2010. The China we knew in 1947/8 is absolutely unrecognisable today. Again, in the book 'Let my people know', Harold Rattenbury tells of his experiences in 1946 when he travelled extensively across China.

Later we were to find that most of the missionaries we met in Hankow had returned to China in 1946. They had worked in China earlier, before the Japanese Invasion, and when the Japanese took over they placed them under house arrest and then in Shanghai warehouse prisons in extremely stressful circumstances. When released they were allowed to go home to England for a furlough, and then to return after a year to their various mission stations in China.

Sunday, 3rd January 1948 - letter from 'TSS Empire Brent' in the Arabian Sea.

Winnie:-

Our voyage through the Suez Canal was most interesting. We arrived at Port Said at 2 a.m. on Sunday morning, (Dec. 28th) and were expecting to be allowed ashore after breakfast so did not trouble to get up. We could hear the winches working above on deck and through the porthole came the cries of the vendors in small boats trying to sell suitcases, handbags (all made of leather), dates, Turkish Delight, etc., so we were a little disappointed when we eventually got up and found the ship already moving out of the harbour. However, it more than made up for our disappointment to go through the canal by daylight. The ship had been fitted with a searchlight in the bows, but this was only needed for a little while during the evening.

We were very surprised to find there were no lock gates at all in the Canal. It is about 80 yards wide and only permits one-way traffic. At regular intervals there were signal stations giving us the right of way. We were only held up once, when several ships passed in the other direction. We passed many villages and, at the point where we stopped, crowds of boys clad only in dirty, long white shirts, came rushing out to greet the boat and clustered around it in small rowing boats. We passed several resting caravans of camels and, at one point, saw an Arab shepherd leading a flock of black sheep. There was a road and railway running alongside the canal for the whole of its length and, at intervals, there were camps for British soldiers (Suez Defence) and RAF stations. A few German POW camps could also be seen.

Just before its end the Suez Canal widens out into two lakes. We have some Roman Catholic Sisters of Mercy on board, going to a hospital in China and before we entered the first lake, we passed a very beautiful Roman Catholic Mission compound with a hospital. Some Sisters of Mercy waved from a balcony and as we entered the lake a launch drew off from the shore with four Sisters aboard. They came on board our ship for a while and greeted the Sisters going to China.

We reached Port Suez in darkness and anchored in the harbour. The town and harbour lights were brilliant. The searchlight from the bows was unloaded and we took on oil and water from tankers, which came alongside, then we left at 6 a.m. just after daybreak. Monday, and part of Tuesday was spent in the Gulf of Suez, which is about 400 miles long. The Red Sea itself is another 1,000 miles in length. In the Gulf of Suez we passed between the mountainous coast of Sinai on one side and the barren hills of Egypt on the other. Once we entered the Red Sea we passed out of sight of land until we went through the Straits at the other end. Throughout, we have had a head-on wind, which has kept the boat steady but on one day caused the waves to break over the foredeck. We turned the corner at the end of the Red Sea and sailed on past Aden on Friday. We should arrive at the Bombay on Tuesday.

Monday evening on 4th January 1948 - same letter.
Winnie:-
Perhaps you would like to hear a little about the various people on board, by this I really mean the cabin life. In my cabin are four children, two boys and two girls aged between 10 and 3 years. Two have been quite ill with tonsillitis during the past week. Then there was a mother with a wee baby of 6 months. The baby was underweight and rather poorly so, when the other children had to be in bed all day, the mother and baby were moved to a cabin on their own. This has worked wonders In many ways. The other people with me are three unmarried missionary ladies and

one wife of a missionary, Mrs Taylor. We often have a long chat for she was living in Bedford for years during the war and knows a number of my friends.

Frank and Winnie
on board TSS Empire Brent

The last two mornings Frank and I have been in charge of a boy named Martin Walker. He is 2 years of age and his mother is disembarking at Bombay. She has another child of 3 months and, being by herself, finds it very difficult to manage in such cramped and crowded conditions.

Today, I tried the typewriter and thoroughly enjoyed using one again, everything is in order and it is a lovely little machine. We have been watching little blue flying fish jump out of the water on either side of the boat, they skim across the surface for fifty to sixty yards.

It is strange in a way, being so remote from the outside world. We receive a Radio Newsletter each morning, which all can read, but it seems so far away. We do hope you are not having the icy weather similar to last winter.

Apart from the food, life on board ship at that time was by no means comfortable or restful. No thought had been given to the needs of young babies and children. Parents relied heavily on the goodwill of their fellow passengers to help supervise and amuse the children during the daytime, especially if they were unwell. Medical facilities were limited to one doctor, who had to rely on other passengers to help should nursing be required. Gertrude Hughes, being a qualified nurse, was called upon once or twice to assist.

Friday, 9th Jan 1948 - letter from 'TSS Empire Brent'.

Frank:-

We have just heard that all letters must be posted on board ship before six o'clock this evening. We should reach Colombo early tomorrow morning and will probably stay there for about six hours. We are in perfectly calm sea and brilliant sunshine. Fortunately, today there is a cooling breeze, yesterday was really very hot, the cabin temperature was about 90°F and over.

Our day in Bombay was very exciting. We berthed on Tuesday evening, instead of Wednesday morning so Winnie and I decided to try and to find somewhere to stay overnight. We quickly obtained visas, changed some money and went ashore. Really, we were most fortunate as we soon found accommodation in a boarding house, many others walked around Bombay for a long time with no success and finally returned to the ship.

When we reached Bombay three weeks had passed and Frank and I were anxious to spend some time on land. The ship was in port for forty-eight hours so we used the time to explore Bombay with Gertrude and the Richardson boys. We enjoyed an ice cream sundae in the Army and Navy Stores, walked and rode around the city in a garry cart. We were deeply moved to see the plight of hundreds of pavement dwellers, each sitting dejectedly beside a bundle of rags that served as their bedding and a tin can used for drinking. It was the turn of 1947/8 and there were thousands of refugees from the Partition, living 'on the street' under makeshift shelters of bamboo sticks hung with pieces of Hessian and leaf matting. We had heard of such poverty but were witnessing it for the first time.

Winnie, Gertrude and the Richardson boys riding on a garry cart Bombay, January 1948.

In deference to the sensitivities of our relatives, we did not describe in our letters home the details of the 'boarding house' accommodation we used for our overnight stay in Bombay. We thought a night alone onshore would be more comfortable than the accommodation on the ship, so once ashore we set about searching for a hotel. Finding a vacant room in a hotel was infinitely more difficult than anticipated, but after looking around we booked into a bed and breakfast establishment. In our haste to explore Bombay we did not bother to inspect the actual accommodation and we were taken aback when we arrived fairly late in the evening and were ushered upstairs into a huge, lofty room furnished with four or five old-fashioned iron bedsteads. Each bed had a thin mattress, one pillow and a couple of cotton sheets, which was quite adequate because the temperature was over ninety degrees Fahrenheit. A wooden partition, about eight feet tall, divided the room in half and on the other side of the partition there were more beds occupied by many other local people who coughed and spluttered all night long. However, the beds were clean and we did manage to get some sleep.

Friday, 9th Jan 1948 - letter from 'TSS Empire Brent' continued -

Frank:-

Bombay looked very beautiful as we arrived. It has a very wide bay and there were hundreds of small and large vessels at anchor. The waterfront was lined with many large, western type buildings, interspersed with Indian buildings, mosques and temples. As we entered the harbour, the sun set behind the buildings in a typically red Indian sunset, quite unlike anything we have ever seen at home.

On Wednesday we had a very exciting, although extremely hot, day going around Bombay. In the morning we went shopping and bought clothing from the European shops. They were fairly well stocked but the prices were terribly high. Winnie bought a pair of shorts and a blouse and I got some cooler shirts. We met Gertrude and the two boys, Tommy and Brian, for coffee and then we hired a 'garry cart', a two-wheeled, horse drawn carriage, to take us around the city. We visited the seafront, saw the native bazaars and finally visited the Zoo.

The native bazaars and the markets were very interesting. Beggars abounded everywhere and there were countless people willing to be guides in order to earn a few annas. We bought fruit from the stalls - there were plenty of oranges and bananas. It was very difficult to get used to the idea of bargaining. It seems to generate such a bad spirit. Our garry cart driver agreed to take us for four rupees an hour, so our fare really came to 10 rupees. He asked for thirty and finally we parted bad friends after we had given him eleven rupees.

This happened all day. The poverty and dirt was very depressing. Apart from the holy men, who lie around in the dust all day long (sometimes in the middle of the road), many from necessity lived on the streets. Their clothing was ragged and worn and, of course, very few possessed footwear. I saw a leper and many of the beggars were obviously ill and some had really bad sores.

The Richardson boys thoroughly enjoyed the day and their excitement gave us a good deal of pleasure. An Indian lad took us around the zoo. He had been born in Trinidad and went to Canaan School. He wore only torn trousers, a shirt and a pair of sandals. He was dirty and looked ill and undernourished. Our way of life is so different, and indeed privileged in comparison, and the Indians were naturally out to make as much money out of us as possible. They were so volatile and easily offended that it was very hard to remain courteous and not overbearing. Tom Richardson says that, while the poverty and squalor in China is often just as bad, we shall not find it so difficult to deal pleasantly with people there as they are altogether more courteous and have a much higher sense of their own dignity and worth as human beings and of the greatness of their national culture. Our next letter should come from Penang or Singapore. We have written to Ban-it-Chiu and hope we shall meet him.

Of course, we now realise that the prickly attitude of the Indian people towards us at that time was due to the fact that they had only recently gained independence from British rule. Whilst on board ship we made friends with the ship's Medical Officer who, on learning that we were newly married, had allowed us to use his cabin to meet if we wished. When we arrived back on board ship after our night on shore we found that we had been moved to the Sick Bay in the stern of the ship. We were the sole occupants of a four berth 'ward' for the rest of the voyage. There was a well-deck for the use of the crew situated between the sick bay and the main deck and each morning when we crossed this to go for our breakfast the crew would ask, 'Are you feeling better today?'

Thursday, 15th January 1948 - letter from 'TSS Empire Brent' between Penang and Singapore.

Frank:-

Colombo was a wonderfully beautiful town, quite unlike Bombay. The streets were much cleaner and the people more cheerful and affluent. We had a really perfect day. The boat anchored in the harbour in the morning and we were allowed ashore about 11:30a.m. We went by launch to the pier, which had quite an imposing foyer advertising Ceylon's tea and beauty. We hired a car to take us all to Mount Lavinia, a beach just outside the town. There were eight of us - Tom and Connie with their two boys and baby, Gertrude, Winnie and myself.

Mt Lavinia was exactly my dream of a tropical beach - a long stretch of golden sand backed by palm trees, a few rocks and a blue, blue sea with small, gentle waves. On the beach were outrigger canoes used for fishing. The canoes are made from hollowed out tree trunks and, to prevent them from upsetting in rough water, they are lashed by crossbars to another long piece of wood lying about 2 yards away from and parallel to them. The natives call them catamarans.

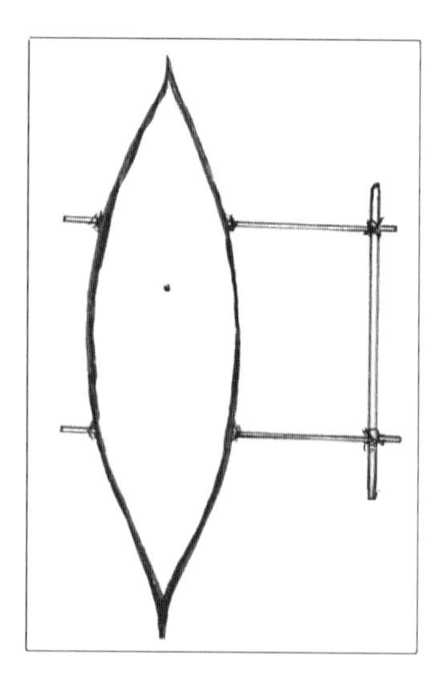

Sketch of a catamaran, as seen in Mount Lavinia, Colombia in 1948 (a novel concept at the time).

<u>Thursday, 15th January 1948</u> - letter contd.

Frank:-

We had lunch in a small hotel, which was situated on a cliff overlooking the beach, and in the afternoon we went bathing. The water was wonderfully warm. Then we had a slow drive back to the ship, eating bananas as we went. We were back on board at 4p.m. and set sail again at 6p.m.

Sunday was an unhappy day for us all. Baby Evatt died and was buried at sea. Mr and Mrs Evatt were wonderfully brave. They were moved into the Isolation Block of the sick quarters to be with Winnie and me and stayed there until we arrived at Penang. (Mr Evatt is taking up work in Penang). The ship's Medical Officer has been extremely good to us both. We two are sharing a very nice four-berth cabin. We sleep in the lower berths and keep our clothes on the top berths. It is terribly hot but we manage with a small fan and keep the door and porthole open.

Throughout the voyage we all enjoyed the good food and relaxed atmosphere, especially as it followed the stringencies and tensions of the wartime and post-war years. The most difficult thing to cope with was the oppressive heat in the unventilated communal cabins and a sad consequence of these conditions was the loss of the young baby Evatt. Perhaps, if I (Winnie) had still been berthed in the large cabin, we would have been aware sooner that the baby boy had become seriously dehydrated. Although Frank and the ship's doctor did all they could to rectify baby Evatt's fluid loss, and the family were moved to a cabin adjacent to ours in the sick bay so that we could keep a very close eye on the baby, we were unable to save him. The ship's doctor kindly allowed the parents to remain in the cabin close to us after the death. They were so distraught. They disembarked at Penang and we often wonder what became of them. We were unable to get their address as they were without one at the time.

Letter of 15th January 1948 continued -

Frank:-

We were in Penang yesterday. We were not allowed ashore. Ban-it came on board to see us. He is still the same 'Bunny' we knew. He is married now and has a two-year-old daughter. He is staying in Penang for five years, then will go back into the ministry, either in Hong Kong, or in England. Ban-it sends you all his love and kind regards.

Chiu-Ban-it, a student friend of Frank's, came on board to meet us at Penang. He brought a huge pineapple and we sat on the deck chatting and eating this gorgeous, juicy fruit. It was the first time we had eaten fresh pineapple.

Chiu-Ban-it on board 'TSS Empire Brent'
14th January 1948

Ban-it later became Bishop in Singapore and after his retirement he came with his wife, Wendy, to live in the New Forest, Hampshire, thus, after 35 years, we renewed contact.

Letter of 15th January 1948 continued -

Penang town lies at the foot of the hills on Penang Island and faces the mainland, which is about a mile away. The railway ends on the opposite side of the mainland, at Prai, but the railway station's booking hall is on the island, the two being connected by a ferry.

The sun set as we left Penang. We passed around the northern end and then down the west coast of the island and now we are sailing close to the Malayan coast. Sumatra can be seen faintly, a long way off, on the opposite side of the ship. We should arrive at Singapore early tomorrow morning and probably we shall go ashore as the boat will be in there all day.

It is 3:45p.m. now. The boat is just passing some small, tree-covered islands. One has a small tower in the middle of it. In a quarter of an hour we shall be having boat drill, we all get our lifebelts and stand near our respective lifeboats. Last night we had another film show on deck. Mummy saw the film with me in Bath - 'The Valley of Decision'. Winnie climbed onto the roof of one of the deckhouses to get a better view. I was following but was stopped by the Master at Arms (the ship's policeman) though Winnie was allowed to stay, so I had a seat in the stalls and Winnie was in the dress circle looking very superior.

We sailed on to Singapore where again, amongst all the colour and clamour, we saw signs of abject poverty. Then onward across the South China Sea to Hong Kong where, on the 23rd of January 1948, we ended our five-week long voyage.

Arrival and stay in Hong Kong - January 23rd to February 2nd 1948

On arrival in Hong Kong we were greeted by Rev Donald Childe, Chairman of the South China District of the Methodist Missionary Society. After gettling us into our accommodation at the Soldiers' and Sailors' Home he informed us that we were to remain in Hong Kong for the time being as the Communists were advancing south and it was considered unwise for anyone to travel up to Hankow immediately. This gave us an unexpected opportunity to explore Hong Kong. It was a city of great contrasts.

The waterfront was lined with huge, flourishing stores selling almost everything one could ever wish to possess, but behind this facade were tiny narrow, noisy, bustling and rather dirty streets, lined with huge tower block tenement dwellings, where each room housed one family. Sanitation was poor, indeed almost non-existent in the tower blocks, and the streets were used as a public toilet resulting in a potent, all-pervading smell of faeces, urine, spices, fruit and dust.

In these back streets one could find little shops and craftsmen working. We have always regretted that we did not purchase one of the beautifully carved camphor wood chests at that time. Alas, although they were relatively inexpensive, we could not afford one, because our savings had been spent equipping ourselves for the five-year stay in China. Never again were we to see such chests for sale.

In 1948 the rail car was climbing to the top of the Peak but unfortunately on the day that we made the trip cloud obliterated the view. At that time the Peak was quite wild and uninhabited, very different from the present day.

We waited in Hong Kong for eleven days and one day we took a bus ride around to the fishing village called 'Aberdeen'. It was a fascinating place, comprising a few houses and hundreds of shipping boats and other vessels on which the community lived. Tiny fish were strewn all over the ground, having been salted or smoked, then laid out on the road to dry in the hot sun. Some folk were making, others mending their fishing nets, whilst others just sat idly by. All of them appeared to us at that time to be poorly nourished and sparsely clothed.

Aberdeen fishing village
Hong Kong
1948.

We spent some time wandering around and then went in search of a meal. We could not utter one word of their language and, although the eating-house had 'restaurant' written in English on its signboard, no member of staff could speak a word of English. Frank took a piece of paper from his shirt pocket and resorted to drawing what he thought looked like a pile of rice on a plate. With much 'Ah-ha-hahing', the waiter disappeared behind a screen. Eventually, he returned bearing two pairs of chopsticks and two dessert-size plates upon which slithered one poached egg apiece. Having no rice and no bread, we literally slurped the eggs up very seriously and bade a courteous farewell.

<u>26th January 1948</u> - letter from Hong Kong.

Winnie:-

We have now been in Hong Kong since last Friday and this is the first opportunity we've had to send a letter. It was a wonderful journey all the way but life on board becomes very limited. We were able to go ashore for a few hours at Singapore. The ship was anchored some distance out and we had our first glimpse of the Chinese town, and its smells. The houses appear to be very overcrowded, but not so dirty and depressing as Bombay. The Chinese shops all open directly onto the road and, when closed, have big shutters across the front. In many streets people sit outside to have their haircut and to eat. The shops are open until about midnight and people never seem to go to bed. There is continual noise all night long. All along these streets are pillars with gaily painted, red and yellow signs. The families live above the shops, and all the houses have verandas where the washing is hung out to dry; this gives a very gay effect and one can almost imagine our streets when we decorate for coronation or something of that sort.

The Chinese parts of Hong Kong are just the same. Preparations are under way for the Chinese New Year, which takes place in about a week's time. Yesterday, we saw some floral decorations being made. It is a joy to see the lovely flowers at this time of year.

The Soldiers' and Sailors' Home is a lovely place. The missionaries have the use of the top floor and the Forces use the rest of the Home. It is a big place and there is no shortage of food. There is a little shop attached, and a restaurant with gorgeous ice creams. This morning, Gertrude and I took the two Richardson boys up to the Peak, 1,190 feet above sea level. From this Peak there is a wonderful view right across the harbour but unfortunately a heavy mist came down whilst we were there and we were unable to enjoy it today. It is terribly cold right up there as the weather in Hong Kong is cold at the moment. I will hand this over to Frank and complete the letter he has been writing to Mother No.2 (Winnie's mother Nellie Hill).

> *Frank:-*
> *Winnie has had a glorious afternoon's shopping while I was seeing about some of the luggage. The shops are full of all sorts of goods unobtainable at home. The prices are about the same, or cheaper, than those at home. Winnie has bought some sheets and wool and is getting*

dress and curtain material. We were a little sorry we bought so much and spent so many coupons at home. Our stay here will probably last about a week - we have to get our goods through customs and obtain a permit for a radio set.

Have you been at all worried about the news from China? Actually, the disturbances at Canton rapidly faded out and the Communist fighting in Central China has not got near to Hankow so we anticipate an uneventful train journey. We should get to Canton in a few hours and then we change stations and get on the train for Hankow - this part of the journey takes 2 - 4 days. We are taking only the very necessary luggage to Hankow, the rest is going to be flown as freight to Chaotung when Elliott Kendall arrives.

Sunday was a thrilling day. We went both to the English Methodist Church and the Chinese Methodist Church.

The Chinese Methodist Church is a magnificent building, built in a triangular fashion. They have to hold two services in the morning to accommodate all the people, and at each service the church is full.

February 12th 1948 - letter from Methodist General Hospital, Hankow.

Winnie:-

It is a long time since we wrote our last really long letter home. We stayed in Hong Kong eventually for eleven days, longer than we thought, but each day seemed to be fully occupied and we were kept quite busy. We had some difficulty in obtaining an entry permit for our wireless, but on the fourth visit we managed to see the 'head man' and he let us have his last permit, which he said he had been keeping for a friend. Tom Richardson did most of the work of obtaining import permits and having our Customs Declaration Form prepared. The Customs regulations are so unjust and exorbitant that the Mission's policy is to make token declarations of things that are definitely dutiable or contraband, such as radios, and leave it to the Customs Officials to tax any additional goods they have a mind to tax. Even so, our duty was quite high (four hundred and twenty-six Chinese dollars at 16 dollars to the pound sterling) and this was for only on one half of our baggage as the Chaotung portion is going to be taken by the Rev Elliot Kendall when he arrives. We should be going by plane to Kunming from Hankow.

Hong Kong is a hilly island, hills rising almost straight from the water to 1200 to 1500 feet. From Hong Kong City there is a tramway running, at times, almost vertically up the hillside to the peak, the highest point of the island. Around the foot of the island are several smaller bays and fishing villages, just offshore and many other smaller islands. A very efficient ferry service connects Hong Kong to Kowloon on the mainland.

Hong Kong was badly damaged and looted during the war but, despite this, great rebuilding and re-equipping has been done and it looks a very prosperous city. We stayed in the Methodist Soldiers' and Sailors' Home. The Home was looted of everything by the Chinese (we now think this was during the liberation of Hong Kong from the invading Japanese), *and only great work by the staff has got it going again. It has now been running again for just a year. It boasts a marvellous restaurant, dormitories, reading room, games room, lounge and chapel, all for the use of British soldiers and sailors stationed In Hong Kong. The top floor is reserved as a guesthouse for missionaries in transit and is being used by all Societies. Hong Kong is now virtually the gateway for the whole of China and we found many interesting people in the Home.*

The Richardson family, Gertrude Hughes, Frank and I, complete with all our baggage, left Hong Kong by train on the 4th of February 1948. I remember how amazed we were to see the coolies, who looked so thin and undernourished, lifting extremely big, heavy crates with utmost ease. I am not sure now exactly how many trunks and wooden packing cases we had with us, but it was a good number. At Victoria Station in Kowloon our baggage was unloaded onto the platform and the customs officials came along to examine it all prior to entry into mainland China.

For us Europeans it was a very long wait and then a tedious procedure to unlock and unscrew our boxes. After the customs search through our belongings the boxes had to be repacked and screwed down once more. But we were treated gently in comparison to the Chinese peasants coming into Kowloon. We witnessed many instances where a bag of precious grain was sliced open with a bayonet, spilling all the contents onto the dirty platform floor.

After this, the poor owner of the bag would spend a long time carefully sweeping up the grain, mending the cloth and making up a fresh bundle.

We realised later that the officials were looking for opium and similar smuggled goods.

Journey from Hong Kong to Hankow

During the train journey from Kowloon to Canton one member of our party sat at all times in the luggage van on guard. On arrival at Canton the luggage was piled up on the platform and we arranged for someone from the travel agency to watch over it for the night while we spent the night at the home of some fellow missionaries. In the morning we boarded a train bound for Hankow. Canton to Hankow was a two night and three day journey, and fortunately, we were able to have a compartment to ourselves. Our main luggage was stowed into a sealed luggage van, while we retained our sleeping bags and a little store of food and drink.

February 12th 1948 letter continued.

Frank:-

We left Hong Kong on Wednesday, February 4th, and went to Canton on the first day. This was only a four and a half hour train journey. We stayed the night in the old Concession Island 'Shamun', which had been the scene of rioting just a little while before. We stayed in the Committee Representative's house, the luggage had to be left in a pile on the platform; if luggage is not constantly watched in China, it will disappear. On the train from Hong Kong to Canton one of us sat on it in the luggage van, along with crowds of Chinese. At Canton it was watched for us over Wednesday night by two of the men belonging to the China Travel Service, but on Thursday night Tom and I took watch in turn. We boarded the Hankow train in the evening, the luggage sealed in a van this time so we had no anxiety about guarding it.

We travelled in a coach that was dilapidated but none-the-less quite comfortable. It was the only first-class coach on the train. China's railways have suffered greatly and need much repair. The track was mostly single line. As we travelled northwards the weather became increasingly colder. In Hunnan we passed through a fall of snow. The first day's journey was through the most beautiful countryside along the West River at the bottom of a wooded gorge. We slept in two berth cabins. The train served two (Chinese) meals a day officially, although on one day there was only one meal, but we amply supplemented this with food rations of our own. There was a constant supply of boiling water, which proved a great boon.

The train was extremely long by our standards and was pulled along by two gigantic steam engines. An attendant supplied boiling water freely throughout the journey, enabling us to make tea when desired. We had been advised to stock up with some tinned food when in Hong Kong.

The train ploughed its way across the vast area between Canton and Hankow. We travelled for miles surrounded by rice fields and other crops, then miles of rather arid grassland. There were few trees to be seen and the landscape was mostly flat. In early February it was quite cold, and the carriages were unheated, therefore we kept our warm clothes on day and night. Because of the risk of bandit attack we were asked to keep our carriage windows blacked-out through the night. Many Chinese people travelled on the roof of the train and at intervals during the daytime we were asked to close the windows while they climbed down to relieve themselves.

On February 7th the huge train huffed and puffed to a halt at Wuchang railway station. Passengers swarmed onto the platform and coolies rushed to collect the baggage. We were met by staff from the Methodist General Hospital, and Mr Heady, Chairman of the District, took us home for breakfast. Noel Richards, a member of the missionary group working at the Methodist General Hospital in Hankow came to escort us by ferryboat across the river Yangtze to Hankow.

In 1948 the River Yangtze and the River Han divided the three cities of Hankow, Wuchang and Hanyang, now known collectively as Wuhan. The ferry crossed the

Yangtze at a point where it was a mile wide, very fast flowing and a muddy yellowish colour. Our luggage was transferred from the train to the ferryboat. This was not without incident for on the way our little cavalcade was halted by a group of soldiers demanding 'Octroi' payment for our goods. Noel Richards, being an 'old China hand', after much argument was able to convince the soldiers that we were only in transit across the country and should not, therefore, be made to pay duty of any kind. We breathed a huge sigh of relief and proceeded on our way.

After the long train journey we were tired and travel worn so I cannot remember much about our first river crossing. After tying up at Hankow we disembarked and were led to a rickshaw. Coolies were lined up ready to deal with our heavy luggage, comprising a couple of cabin trunks and about six large, heavy, wooden crates. They hung these in rope nets on two poles, then two coolies, one in front of the crate the other behind, placed the ends of the poles on their shoulders and started to trot through the streets and alleyways. Once in their stride they called out to warn the thronging pedestrians to move out of the way. We followed them in our rickshaw.

Everywhere people stared at us in wonder. Strange 'red' people, such as us, had rarely been seen entering their city for many years. Riding through the city streets we were surrounded by a cacophony of banging gongs and people calling out to sell their wares. Almost every shop seemed to possess a loudspeaker emitting loud vocal music. We travelled a couple of miles through streets lined with shops: butchers, fruiterers busily flicking away flies in an effort to fend off flies, cloth merchants displaying lengths of beautiful, brightly coloured silks, and here and there a teashop. We passed grocers, tailors, tea sorters, tea drinkers, and shops where firecrackers could be purchased. Sometimes we caught sight of a huckster beating his drum as he walked along announcing the contents of his bundle.

As we got past the outskirts of the vast city the houses were large and well built, the roads wider and well made but, gradually, as we entered the busy central area the streets became much narrower and very dirty. Small, open-fronted shops, with tables and benches set out on the cobblestones served hot soup and noodles to their customers. Approaching the Hospital the street became so narrow that the coolies had to push people aside in order to keep moving.

Throughout the city, large transverse blocks of granite were placed along each road, to cover the central drain, which contained all the wastewater from shops and houses. This dirty, smelly mess oozed its way into the river lower down. There were no other drains. Human excreta was carried from various collecting pits, in open buckets down to the dung boats, ready to be rowed to the surrounding rural areas, where it was transferred into huge cess pits and later spread on the vegetable fields. The whole situation of thousands of human beings crowded into a limited space resulted in a very special 'odour' recognisable in many big cities the world over, especially during the hot season. When reading this please do not forget that these were the conditions in the late 1940's since which much has improved in sewage disposal, clean water supplies and road and rail transport.

Returning to 1948 - The entrance to the Methodist General Hospital was a very wide doorway which opened into a small courtyard. We alighted from the rickshaw, walked up a couple of steps and passed through another wide doorway, into the Entrance Hall where the Medical Superintendent and some of his staff gave us a wonderful welcome. This official welcome completed we left the Hospital and proceeded to our living quarters.

We were led through a small alleyway opposite the hospital entrance. Along the way stood a coldwater tap around which were a group of women, some collecting buckets of water, others washing clothes, and others vegetables, while some were just gossiping. The majority of houses had no private access to water. Along each side of the pathway ran a smelly, slimy, green stream of water-cum-urine that trickled its way down to the river Han at the end of the alley.

Orientation in HANKOW - mid-February to June1948

The entrance to the Methodist General Hospital, Hankow in 1948.

We turned left through a gateway set in a fairly high brick wall, which surrounded the Mission Compound, and found ourselves in a completely different world. The wall encompassed a collection of four really large, airy houses, each set in a small garden. This is where the missionary personnel lived, protected from the outside world, behind the compound gate that could be locked for safety against intruders. In years gone by there had been violent attacks on foreigners so this was more than just a wish for privacy.

In one of the compound houses lived Dr. Arthur Russell, his wife Doris and their two children, Brian and Barbara. Arthur and Doris looked after us throughout our six-month stay in Hankow, whilst we began our language study lessons and were introduced to the ways and customs of the Chinese people.

Winnie looking at the view of the River Han from the Russells' balcony.

Hankow, being low lying and situated in the centre of China, is subject to extremes of temperature. During the winter the temperature drops below freezing, whereas in the summer months it can reach 104°F with up to 75 per cent humidity. The mission houses were large, well ventilated and relatively cool during the summer, but during the winter it was necessary to wear our warmest clothing indoors - a Chinese padded gown, mittens and boots - because, apart from a charcoal stove in one room, the house was not heated at all.

February 9th and 10th 1948 - letter from Hankow.

Frank:-

We arrived at Wuchang on Sunday morning, February 7th, at 7am Hankow is really the name given to one third of this great city. The other parts are Wuchang and Hanyang. They are separated by the Yangtze and Han rivers.

The river here rises about 90 feet in the rainy season and has steep banks. It is wide and in places packed with junks of all sizes, each junk having a whole family living on board.

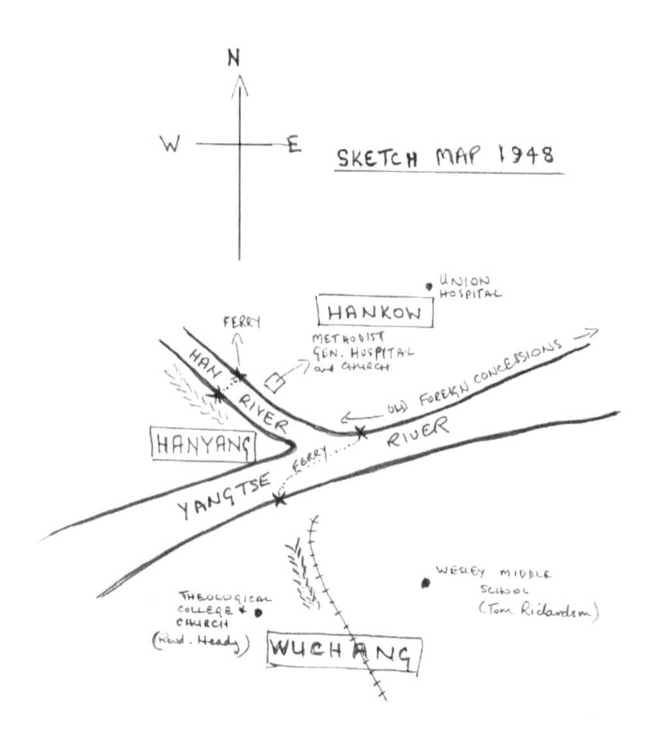

Plan of the rivers that divided Hankow, Hanyang and Wuchang.

The Chairman of the District, the Rev Heady, welcomed us at Wuchang and we had breakfast with him. He is living in the Church and Theological College compound, which was used as a Red Cross hospital during the war and was badly damaged.

After breakfast Rev Noel Richards took us over the Yangtze by ferryboat and on to the Methodist General Hospital In Hankow. We rode with some of our baggage in rickshaws and the rest came on later by coolies. At the Methodist General we are staying with one of the two English doctors, Arthur Russell and his wife. Arthur is about 34 and has been out here for eight years. He was interned in Shanghai and has since been home and taken his M.D. in Tropical Medicine. They are really charming people and have made us thoroughly at home. We have a large bedroom to ourselves and have been able to unpack all our goods.

So far Arthur has taken us around the General Hospital and we have paid a visit to the Union Hospital. The Chinese Superintendent of the General Hospital is coming to England for a time in a few days time. His name is Dr Chiang and during the war he did a marvellous job keeping the hospital going. Dr Cundall, the Superintendent of the Union, is coming over here to take charge. His son Bob is engaged to Monica Pritchard, daughter of the late Rev Pritchard who was Chairman of the Cornwall District. I met him at the London Hospital. Andrew Pearson is the other English doctor at the General Hospital and Daddy may remember meeting him on a train from Bedford. At the moment he has gone on a short holiday to visit his parents.

Our programme has not yet been worked out. I expect we shall be going to the Union Hospital for Surgery and Midwifery. There is a very good senior surgeon there named Gillison and a younger surgeon, Heath Thompson, who does the midwifery. At the General we shall probably work with Arthur and he will teach me tropical diseases and help me revise general medicine. We have already done a ward round with Arthur and have seen several patients with him. As yet, we have not arranged a language teacher, but hope to do so soon.

Yesterday, we were given a welcome party. Arthur's wife, Doris, is a wonderful cook and she excelled herself. Nearly all the mission turned up and we had great fun playing party games. Tonight, we are going to Dr Chiang's house for a Chinese dinner. Winnie and I had some practice with chopsticks in Hong Kong and on the train but our proficiency isn't yet very high. Next week there is going to be a big combined official welcome for us and Dr. Cundall and a farewell to Dr Chiang.

Our wedding photographs arrived on Monday by airmail, and it was a great joy to get them. Now I'm considerably fatter and look quite a different picture. In our next letter we'll tell you about the hospitals and the work here. Until then, we send our love and hope you will keep well.

We began a routine of individual language study for an hour each every day. A sweet, petite lady, named Miss Wu, came to the house and she was so patient with our stumbling efforts.

After language study we would go to the Methodist General Hospital or walk around the city. Across the city was a second hospital, 'The Union', reached by a pathway running alongside the railway lines. We often visited The Union, I to learn some physiotherapy and Frank to help in the operating theatre.

When walking there in the early morning we would see dead bodies left lying on the railway embankment. We were told that those who could not afford a proper burial for a relative would make do with placing the body on a raised piece of land. Another practice, new to us, was the placing of a newborn baby by the hospital doorstep, or just outside our compound gateway, in the sure knowledge that it would be taken in and cared for. Babies were also often left at the Buddhist Temples for the same reason.

Thinking back now I realise how much we had to observe, absorb and learn during the first few weeks after our arrival. Many customs were quite different from our own. For instance: 'When a friend calls always first offer tea and sunflower seeds and, whilst sipping the tea and cracking the seeds, talk about family matters, the weather etc., for about ten minutes.' It was only after such formalities had been observed that one should ask the reason for the visit, or the guest would tell you why he or she had come.

This kind of etiquette was still in use when we visited China in 1981 and 1984, when, although all the hospital visits had been pre-booked, on arrival at the hospital there would be a reception party standing outside the main entrance ready to escort us into a large meeting room where we would all sit around a table sipping tea and making small talk before the hospital official business could begin.

<u>Thursday, February 12th 1948</u> - extracts from a letter from Hankow

Winnie:-

I believe the news you are getting outside is rather alarming, especially as regards Central China, but in actual fact there is little to alarm you as far as Hankow is concerned. The work is going on as usual and, though we are watching the Communist Army's moves, we do not anticipate any advance here. Tuberculosis is very rampant here and there is no means at all of treating it.

We are virtually millionaires - prices are rising every day - 1 million Chinese dollars is now worth about £2.

While living in Hankow we travelled across the Yangtze River on the ferryboats from Hankow to Wuchang and back several times, however familiarity did not steady the nerves. The first trip I have forgotten but not so the later experiences. First of all we purchased tickets, then joined a crowd of two to three hundred other would-be passengers waiting behind huge, locked, metal gates on the riverside. As the ferryboat, an old landing craft, approached people started to press forward, all anxious to get on board. When the gates were eventually opened there was a terrific surge of bodies, boxes, and bundles of every size and description, and we were literally swept on board amidst a sea of people. This was pretty frightening the first time. The boats were quite large and would be filled to capacity with standing room only and the ferryboat just, only just, floating above the waterline. The current of the River Yangtze at this mile wide stretch is frighteningly swift. The ferry was launched and slowly it chugged upstream against the current for a mile or so, then with engines at full pelt, it swirled crazily across the river to the opposite bank.

Another ferryboat ran from Hankow to Hanyang and this was a much less traumatic undertaking. Winnie was happy to cross this part of the river with Doris Russell and children.

February 12th 1948 - extract from a separate letter to Frank's father.

Frank:-

We think of you often and hope that you will have succeeded in your last valiant attack on the Contact Lens examination. We really are very grateful to you for all you are doing for us.

(It is interesting to note here the date of the advent of contact lenses. Frank's father, Ernest, qualified to prescribe them when they were first made available.)

February 20th 1948 - letter from Hankow.

Winnie:-

On Monday, we started our language study with the Chinese teacher, Miss Wu, who lives on the compound. It is great fun making all sorts of peculiar noises and knowing very little of the meaning. Our lessons are from 9 to 10am and 3 to 4pm each day. So far we have learnt 有没有 *'you mung you', which means literally 'have not have', and* 不 *'buh', which means 'not' when in use with 'want' and so on.*

After the morning language lesson we go to General Hospital outpatients department. This is most helpful. Already we have seen many interesting cases, leprosy, malaria, typhoid, lung abscess etc., and lots of tuberculosis, these latter being in-patients. We go round the wards with Arthur Russell and now, today, Dr Rao has called Frank over to see one or two of his patients. Andrew Pearson has called him also.

There was a Clinical Meeting at the hospital on Wednesday evening and Frank gave a lecture on Empyema. We are both free to come and go almost as we like. At the moment I am trailing round with Frank trying to learn as much as possible in order to be useful in Chaotung. We have thought that it would be best if I learn something about hospital management out here and also how to give anaesthetics, as well as outpatient work; in this way, I shall have no fear of overstepping the nurses' duties.

Doris Russell has kindly offered to give me some idea as to cooking the different types of food one gets in China. Her cook makes bread and such like and will give me a lesson in making yeast from potatoes. We are sure that this time will prove invaluable for our future work.

Sunday February 22nd - same letter continued.

Frank:-

Our work at the General Hospital is now fairly well organised and I am just waiting to hear when we ought to go to the Union Hospital. The common diseases here are quite different from those at home. The rare ones at home are the commonest here. In a way, one has to learn medicine all over again. The frequency of endemic tropical diseases adds considerably to the possible diagnoses for each case. The missionaries here are living in quite western style houses and we are eating Western food except that, in place of potatoes we eat rice.

In my next letter I will describe the buildings that lie on the N. E. side of the main street. These include the Outpatient Department, Men's Wards, Nurses' Home and Chapel. The main street is always crowded with people. It is no wider than Union Passage in Bath and covered with uneven paving stones with areas of mud in between. On a rainy day we have to wear Wellington boots. Occasionally a car may find its way bumping up the street, but mostly, there is a long string of rickshaws and a jostling crowd. All the shops open straight onto the streets and have no glass fronts at all.

I am getting to know the Chinese doctors here. Andrew Pearson arrived back on Sunday - we went for a walk together yesterday afternoon along the bund of the river. The riverbanks are packed with small boats of all descriptions. There are quite a number of refugees from the Communist areas. The river at the moment is low. It rises and falls about 90ft each year. We are just coming to the end of the cold weather and spring seems to be on its way. Already we have had to make plans for our summer holiday. We are going with the Russell's to Kuling, a hill resort, which is very cool after the heat of the Yangtze valley.

Hankow was an extraordinary and fascinating city. It was divided into two parts. One part, called the Cantonment, boasted wide asphalt roads, pavements on which to walk, covered drains and large, beautiful houses set in huge compounds. It was occupied by foreign diplomats and businessmen and here people would sit on the lawns under the shelter of large, shady trees and enjoy cucumber sandwiches served with afternoon tea whilst a small orchestra played quietly in the background.

An afternoon in the park, Hankow.

The other part of the city did possess a few wide streets with open sewer drains about three and a half feet deep and thirty inches wide. These ran along their length threatening to trip the unwary pedestrian, especially during the hours of darkness. This part of Hankow was crammed full of people living in the most squalid conditions, literally on the street, or in dwellings of every description, huge tenement blocks, tiny rickety shacks, the whole intersected with narrow, cobblestone streets which smelt of urine and excrement. Along the Ta Ma Lu, the main street, which ran across the end of the General Hospital Road, rickshaws, pony carts, carrying coolies, lorries, buses, bicycles, hand drawn carts and pedestrians were to be seen, all hurrying along with hooters blowing, bells ringing, people shouting and merchants crying out their wares - altogether a terrific noise and sight. Rickshaws were the common mode of travel for foreigners and the richer Chinese citizens. Many patients arrived at outpatients in rickshaws and sedan chairs were rarely seen. Most goods were transported in large carts pulled by a coolie, or suspended by ropes from a bamboo pole carried across the shoulders.

March 15th 1948 - letter from Hankow.
Winnie:-
For the past five days we have had heavy rain and the rivers are rising rapidly. We were told that this sort of weather continues for about a month and then the warm weather comes to stay. Hankow district is very low lying and there is thick mud and water everywhere. Our gumboots are most useful. Yesterday, when we went round the wards it was a huge joke; Arthur Russell was wearing a white coat with mack on top and gum boots, Frank had a long flowing theatre gown on and was carrying his umbrella. I wore an equally long, flowing theatre gown and gumboots. We wondered what would be said if we did a ward round dressed in such attire in England.

Last Monday we had a grand sort out with regard to our programme. We were finding that the amount of time set aside for language study was nowhere near enough and so, after a long talk with Dr Cundall, we acted on his advice and now time is spent as follows. Every day, apart from Thursday and Friday, we do language study from 9am until 4.30pm, Thursday and Friday we go to the Union Hospital for the surgical ward round and theatre work. Last week we put four plasters on and I (Winnie) was in my element. I am going to learn something about massage and breathing exercises from Mrs Thompson at The Union. We think this will be most useful at Chaotung for fractures and postoperative cases, at present they have nobody on the staff with knowledge of this sort.

An item of news about Chaotung - the other day we received a letter from Dr Galbraith saying that she had obtained permission to engage a second Chinese doctor owing to the large amount of work to be done. She has so far been unable to contact one and asked us to inquire in Hankow. It just happens that at the moment there is a very nice Chinese intern at the Methodist Hospital here, Dr Wong, he is thought much of and is a good Christian young man so we told him about the hospital in Chaotung. After thinking the matter over, he has decided to come and join us soon after we should arrive. His home is in the same district and we do hope he will be happy with us. He comes to see us every Monday evening in the hope that we can teach him some English. Actually, he knows quite a lot and is teaching us a lot of Chinese medical terms. He is just the sort of person we had hoped to be working with, and once again we thank God for the wonderful way in which he provides for us.

I am getting a lot of requests to teach nurses English and also piano playing. On Sunday afternoons Frank, Andrew Pearson and I go along to the Chinese church and have a musical session. Andrew plays the violin and I the piano, I also sing, we have a wonderful time.

Now we have a new toy to play with. On Friday, we brought our battery back from the Union Hospital where it had been charged. As soon as we arrived home we set about fitting up the wireless. It goes well and we heard Sandy Mac at the theatre organ last night. We were surprised to find, on hearing the news, how much we had missed. In fact some of the items meant nothing to us. I expect we shall sort them out soon now we can get news regularly.

On our walks to the Union we passed rows of wood and matting huts. Whole families live in these huts, which are no bigger than a large room in our houses at home. Some of them are almost standing in water. They mostly belong to farmers whose rice fields are becoming a most vivid and lovely green. The trees are beginning to bud and the grass is turning green as well. It is a grand sight, so much brighter than at home.

March 21st 1948 - letter from Hankow.

> *Frank:-*
>
> *It has been a wonderful day. As it is Palm Sunday, Winnie and I were just going to read the Moravian Readings for the day, when in came the boy with a pile of letters. We have had none for a fortnight because of the heavy rains. The river is already many feet higher. No planes have got through from Shanghai until yesterday.*
>
> *Now that the rains have arrived the temperature has dropped considerably. Winnie and I have been glad of our ex-army things. Mummy's mittens too have been very welcome. Now Doris has provided a small study for us and we have a charcoal fire on an open pan set in the middle of the room. The electricity supply is cut off during the daytime and only comes on at night, so it is a good thing that we brought a wet battery for the wireless. Dr Galbraith tells us that the Chaotung electricity supply is even more unreliable. We are very glad of John's storm lantern. We have two spare batteries still so it should last us this year.*
>
> *Winnie is very pleased with the sewing machine. It runs so quietly. At first she was very puzzled by the fact that it seemed to sew backwards until she found a reversing lever and made it go forward. It is going to be a great asset to us.*

This Singer Sewing Machine, hand driven, was given to me (Winnie) as a wedding present from staff at the Bedford County Hospital. It was shipped back home when Frank left China. We took it to Mysore, in South India, where it did valiant service throughout our stay. 'Tata', as we used to respectfully call the elderly gentleman tailor, periodically came and sat on the veranda for a couple of weeks and made all our clothes. When we left India in 1966 we gave the sewing machine to him.

Frank continues:-
The inflation here is quite a complicating factor in life. During the last week the Chinese dollar has changed from nine thousand Chinese dollars to the pound sterling, to one million, four thousand. The prices of goods have not risen quite as steeply. We are all paid at the rate of three hundred pounds sterling a year, plus a bonus, the bonus having a ceiling of one hundred per cent. Each month the bonus is worked out from an index based on the cost of rice and other staple commodities. Whatever we are paid here, eighty pounds sterling is being sent back home each year to go on to our Mission House account for savings and home expenses.

Heath Thompson, the Friends Ambulance Unit surgeon at the Union, is going to England in six weeks. He is a New Zealander, but he wants to take his FRCS before going home. Bob McClure, FRCS, an older man, has come out to take his place. He is a Canadian and destined for the London Missionary Society in Honan, but he cannot go there because of the Communists. We had a very enjoyable ward round with him on Thursday and I'm looking forward to working with him. We have already booked a case of prolapsed intervertebral disc and hope to do it when the diathermy set is working.

I am finding that quite a number of cases are arriving to see me in the General Hospital now. I was called three times this week to see some cases presenting unusual features. Peter Hoin, one of the surgeons, asked me to do a ward round with him to give him more recent teaching about his cases. Yesterday, there were three empyemas cases to drain. By coincidence all had a history of 1 month's illness, all were boys aged 6, 7 and 8, and they all had left sided empyemas.

Winnie wrote to Dr Galbraith asking for advice about any special work she could train for which would be of use in Chaotung. Heath Thompson's wife has built up a physiotherapy school at the Union and has offered to give Winnie some teaching during the few weeks she has left in China. Dr Galbraith thinks this would be useful. Winnie is also learning to give anaesthetics and she hopes to learn some laboratory work when I am doing some in the summer. There will also be quite a lot of bookkeeping to do when we get to Chaotung. Winnie gave the anaesthetics for the empyema yesterday.

On Good Friday and Easter Sunday Winnie is singing in a quartet at the Chinese church. On Tuesday, Dr Dousiell at the Union is giving a gramophone recital of the whole of the 'Messiah'. We hope to go over in the evening at 7 p.m. It will finish after 10 o'clock and he is going to bring us back in their ambulance.

<u>Letter continued Tuesday evening.</u>

I don't remember having told you anything about our food here. Apart from one or two Chinese meals a week we live on food just like that we get at home, except we eat rice in place of potatoes and have a few different vegetables such as water lily root, bean shoots, celery-like cabbage and Chinese spinach. The Chinese meals are great fun. Usually there is a round table seating about ten persons, the seats are tall square-topped stools. The chief guests are given the seats of honour facing the door. As a rule the host orders a different dish for each guest and the total number of people present; if ten people, ten dishes plus a large bowl of soup. The food is mostly chopped up into small pieces and fried, each dish is brought to the table separately and piping hot. The host lifts his chopsticks from the table and points to the dish in the centre saying 'Ching', and then we all commence to eat. The correct

thing to do is to take one or two portions and after eating them put down the chopsticks, talk to your neighbour and wait for the next course. It is considered bad manners to eat the whole dish of food.

These meals take anything from one to two hours, usually the latter, but they are interesting and most enjoyable. One way of serving up the leftover dishes is to mix them up together with noodles (long ribbons like macaroni) and serve as a soup. This is called 'mein', an ideal meal for a cold night.

April 7th 1948 - letter from Hankow

Winnie:-

Many apologies for not writing last week. Time simply flies and even so we do not seem to do as much work as we should like. Actually we are progressing very well with language study and Frank is able to do quite a lot of medical and surgical work.

During the last week it has been just like an English summer, we have started wearing our summer clothes; this sort of temperature lasts until the end of May and then it really becomes hot. The women and children reckon to go to Kuling sometime during June or early July and I am expected to go with them. I'm not very anxious to go at the moment but I expect, when the hot weather arrives, it will prove to be the best plan.

The poor men have to stay in Hankow longer. Frank will not leave until the end of July. When we return to Hankow in September we shall have to pack ready to go to Chaotung.

All the hospitals are kept very busy. We've just received last year's report on the work at Chaotung and it makes most interesting reading. They cover a tremendous amount of work, especially the Maternity Department. The type of people found there are different from those living around Hankow. They are much more primitive, poor and dirty but nevertheless they need as much, and as careful treatment, if not more so. Frank is finding the hospital work here most helpful and is constantly coming across things he's never done or seen before.

On Easter Monday we took a day off and went with a party to visit 'the graves'. We all set off fairly early in the morning and went right along the road, which runs parallel to the River Han, for about two miles (I'm not absolutely sure about the distance but it was a good way), then we crossed the river and so on to Hanyang. The graves stretch for miles and miles across the countryside.

The main entrance to the Methodist Church, Hankow.

The Methodist Church in Hankow has two sections, one older, and when full the other is also used. We held a service at each section. The Chinese people were there also.

After service we walked a little way and then had some lunch. Beyond the graves is a stretch of farmland, where water stands in pools all over the place. Narrow, raised paths run between the pools, and in the pools live hundreds of frogs. They croak all day and all night and yet it is most difficult to see them. Tadpoles are sold on the streets in little round glass containers about two inches in diameter.

We set off for home at about 5pm and travelled all the way down the river in a small boat. There were two boatloads and we had a race. Cambridge won! The children thoroughly enjoyed the fun as the boat that started last, arrived first.

On Sunday there was a big service for the nurses' graduation. The nurses were all dressed in white and wore lovely buttonholes. The church was beautifully decorated with flowers. On the platform there were about eight 'official' people, and the French Consul's wife presented the Certificates. Various people made speeches and the nurses sang a special graduation song. It must be a great day for most of them as it is a magnificent achievement. The standard of nursing is quite high and it is a great thing to realise that the majority of them are Christian girls.

I think perhaps Frank would like to add a note if he has time so I will leave some space.

Continued April 8th

Frank has no time to complete this today as Arthur has been called to an urgent case in Wuchang and Frank is to do his X-ray session. It is rather difficult to fit these in as the electricity supply is cut off from 10am to 6pm, and all outpatients come back to hospital in the evening for X-ray examinations. Frank sends his love to you all. Winnie

April 11th 1948 - letter from Hankow.

Frank:-

It is about 3 weeks now since I have written to you myself, Winnie has had to deputise for me. Our days are very full, yet we seem to do only a fraction of what we plan. The climate is very variable at the moment. One day it is 90°F in the shade and then, in a few hours, a terrific wind and rainstorm develops and the next day it is about 30°F or more cooler. As a result, we can only do a small amount of the work we used to do in England. We steadily progress with our language study. It is a matter of constant practice, forgetting and relearning again and again until finally we remember the words and characters, but we both find it great fun. It is a thrill to find we can make ourselves understood.

I have been getting quite a number of chest cases referred to me - the six months in the London Chest Hospital are proving most helpful. In the Children's Ward, I have five little children with Empyemas. Some are doing well now though they have had their ups and downs, but two are giving us quite a lot of worry. Last week I made a plaster bed for one of the nurses who developed a TB spine. Winnie is going to see her every day for exercises and massage. Our visits to the Union Hospital are very valuable. Bob McClure has joined the staff at Union Hospital, he has considerable experience with radium and I'm learning quite a lot from him. Last weekend it was the 20th Anniversary of the founding of the Union Hospital and on Sunday the first big post-war Graduation Ceremony of the nurses. This was an impressive ceremony. The church was packed with visitors and prettily decorated with flowers. The graduating nurses were in the choir stalls and came, one by one, to receive their graduation certificates.

April 13th 1948 - letter from Hankow continued.

Winnie:-

Frank is very sorry that he is unable to finish this letter himself but has asked me to do so instead. This weekend we have been to stay with Tom and Connie Richardson in Wuchang. The Middle School is situated out in the country and just behind Tom's house is a large stretch of fields and then hills in the distance. On Saturday, we went for a long walk to the Pagoda Hill and climbed right up inside the pagoda. They are built very solidly and the stairs are quite steep and wind round and round to the top. At intervals there are little domed rooms with steps leading outwards to small windows. The view from the top was wonderful and one could see for miles right across the valley.

Wuchang University
1948.

Yesterday we received two letters, one from each home. You would just love travelling around here John. Every time one gets into any vehicle one takes a risk, rickshaws are very rickety indeed. The horse-drawn carriages are often almost falling to pieces, and occasionally a wheel comes off. Always these vehicles are piled high with people sitting and standing, they go dashing along the road sending everything and everybody scattering before them. Then come the buses. You know the dilapidated old crocks that one sees on the rubbish heap at home - well - one of

those on wheels; no glass in the windows; wooden seats around the inside edge and, in the centre standing room; put forty people in it and there is a Chinese bus. Often there is a mechanic sitting on one side of the bonnet holding two pieces of wire together whilst the bus goes bumping and crashing along the rough road.

Frank and I have travelled in one on two occasions and if you're not early enough to get a seat then you just stand with the others around holding you up. When you reach your destination you push, wriggle and squeeze until finally, with one big, deep, breath, you fall out. In spite of this sometimes two get out and four pile in with baskets and bundles hanging from the windows. What fun!

April 15th 1948 - letter from Hankow.

Winnie:-

Frank and I sometimes take a shortcut to the Union Hospital. The path runs alongside the railway line. Although we have been the same way two or three times it was only last week that we discovered the significance of the wooden boxes which lie strewn all along the bank. Last week there were about thirty such boxes, and actually they are coffins. Some are old and broken, containing just skeletons, others are comparatively new and contain bodies ready for burial. Evidently the poor people use this place as a dumping ground, they say it costs a lot of money for funerals.

April 25th 1948 - extract from letter.

> *Frank:-*
>
> *We've had another interesting week. We went over to the Union Hospital on Wednesday and Thursday mornings, and Winnie made a third visit on Friday. She is making the best of the last few days that Bunny Thompson has in China to learn as much physiotherapy as possible.*

May 16th 1948 - extracts from letter from Hankow.

Frank:-

The Chinese have just introduced air letter forms, which can be sent from inside China, as distinct from Hong Kong, before long you will be receiving some from us. The paper is very poor and won't take ink so Winnie will be typing them.

We are all making advanced plans for our stay in Kuling, deciding what stores we ought to get and take with us. Kuling is one day's journey by steamer down the river Yangtze then a rough journey by truck overland and a two hour climb up the hill to follow. The women and children are usually carried up in chairs.

We have been having heavy rain and the paddy fields are all flooded. Some of the footpaths in the low-lying ground around the Union Hospital are underwater. The river has risen considerably - about forty feet - and from our bedroom window we can see the water clearly, whereas before we could only see the tops of the boats. The mosquitoes are now getting busy and we have put our net up over the bed.

The Russell's have been given a little kitten and Winnie has taken special charge of it. The three Cram children, who live next door to us, have measles. Winnie goes in to help bath them every morning.

Yesterday we had a very delightful outing. We packed a picnic lunch (spoilt by my using rancid butter by mistake) and went across the river Yangtze towards Wuchang. We took a bus out to East Lake, to the University, which lies on its shores. It is one of the few wooded areas around here and is a really delightful spot. We could see opposite us some of the hills of Hunan and the lake is so vast that one can hardly see the other shore.

Continued May 23rd

We had two Chaotung nurses, who are here studying midwifery, to supper this week. They were very nice girls, rather shy and quiet. Their accent is quite different from the Hankow. We learned more about the types of cases that we shall meet in Chaotung. There is a good deal of midwifery to be done. I am still doing eyes and midwifery with a little ssurgery and am going round the surgical wards with the surgeons. My lung abscess case has had several secondary haemorrhages and had to be transfused twice - I do hope he will survive. All the empyemas are doing well now. I made an anterior plaster bed for our nurse with T.B.spine about fifteen days ago but the weather has been so hot and damp that, even now, it is not dry and has begun to grow whiskers. We have packed away all our winter clothes now, they would grow whiskers too if left out.

Tomorrow I'm going to try a plastic operation on a very advanced ectropion that is too bad for any of the more simple operations. There is also an optical iridectomy to do. Trachoma is the cause of 90% of the eye infections.

Yesterday was very hot and Winnie and I stoutly pedalled some borrowed bicycles along the riverbank to a place called 'Seven Mile Creek'. It was an attractive, boat-building village. We made a meal of some bananas and oranges and then we met an Army Officer who could speak some English. He, with the traditional (but not customary) Chinese courtesy, invited us to the Officers' Mess where we rested a while, chatted and drank boiled water.

June 9th 1948 - letter (typewritten) from Hankow

Winnie:-

Frank is again taking the Medical Meeting tonight. They are discussing theatre work. I am in the midst of packing for Kuling. Doris Russell and the children are going on Friday and taking the servants with them, so I have to go too. It is a great disappointment for us, as we had hoped to travel up together at the end of the month, however we must not be selfish.

(Once I did the journey I realised how confusing we would have found it had we gone by ourselves with our miniscule knowledge of the language.)

Last weekend, we went to Shih Wei Yao. It is situated about eighty miles down the river Yangtze. At 3.30am on Friday morning we arose from our beds and had a quick breakfast. The cook and boy joined us and we all piled into rickshaws at 3.45am and went to the ferry. We boarded a launch at 4.30am. There was hardly any room on board, the boat was absolutely crammed with people. We were taken down under at the stern of the boat and had to stand for quite awhile until gradually the people sleeping on the floor were roused by one of the launch hands and we all moved around to create a little more sitting space along the edges of the deck. After that, those of us left standing took it in turns to sit on the floor in the middle of the deck area where it was terribly hot and stuffy, or stand by the portholes where there was a breeze.

I remember that at the time I was wearing European style dress and our fellow Chinese travelling companions kept peeking under my skirt to make sure that I was covered underneath. I had been warned to wear knickers with elastic top and bottom.

We had taken no food or drink with us as we understood it was brought round. Unfortunately, a lot of soldiers had come on board at the last minute, which meant that there was insufficient food to go around. We therefore had nothing to eat or drink until we arrived at our destination at 3pm. Of the countryside en route we saw very little as you can imagine. However, as soon as we arrived at Shih Wei Yao we were met by Andrew Pearson and Edith Milner and our luggage was taken off in the hospital rickshaw whilst we made a hurried dive into a Chinese restaurant. There, we ate fried rice and shrimps. Oh boy, was it good! By the way, I should have told you that we went with Bob McClure, an 'old hand' in this kind of situation. Having satisfied the 'inner man' we made our way to the hospital. It is a very nice building situated at the foot of the hills. It is possible to walk out of the back door and straight up the hillside. What a difference after Hankow! Once there, we had tea, then followed an inspection of the electricity and water supplies. They want to build some extensions to the hospital buildings and Bob was sent to investigate. After supper, we went for a short walk up the hillside, then to bed at eight thirty, and slept soundly until six o'clock the next morning. The temperature is in the 90°Fs now, so you can guess we were all pretty tired.

After breakfast on Saturday morning, we went to see the coal mine, the ironworks and another hospital, where they have the most wonderful equipment. There are three Chinese doctors on the staff. It is depressing to see this very modern apparatus that cannot be used for lack of skilled personnel. Back for lunch and then off for a visit to the new cement works that is being built. It is a tremendous place having two kilns each eleven foot six inches in diameter. It was a most interesting expedition. With all this development in the district the question of our Hospital equipment and its staff is quite important as, when the cement works gets going properly, there will be plenty of work, together with the other two industries. Whilst we were at the cement works a party of bank managers from Hankow were being shown around and they gave us a lift back to the hospital in their truck. Frank started talking to one of them and asked when they were going back to Hankow. He replied, 'Tomorrow. When are you?' Frank said, 'Tomorrow,' and immediately we received an offer to go back on the Company's launch at 8am on Sunday. After tea, we went to the storeroom of the hospital and made a list of instruments in theatre and the new things wanted. My typing came in useful for once. Bob McClure remained in Shih Wei Yao.

The trip back was wonderful. We had every comfort; armchairs to sit in, Chinese feasts and good company. The group of men on board were most interesting to talk to and the day passed in a pleasant, restful way. The countryside all the way down the river is quite hilly with little villages here and there and occasionally, quite a large town. We were not told the names of these places. The contact made with these men has resulted in the Director of the bank wanting to meet Bob and some others of our Mission to talk over the question of medical care of their employees.

The reason for the feast was that the bankers had given some money to the cement company. We had fish, chicken, beef, pork and all sorts of other things (about seven courses for lunch, and another seven for our evening meal). The meat is chopped into small pieces, cooked in a variety of sauces and served on a number of small dishes, which are placed in the centre of the table around a huge bowl of piping hot soup.

Poor Frank still gets stuck occasionally when trying to manipulate his chopsticks. I seem to manage fairly well. I am more afraid that Frank is not getting enough to eat, but we ate Chinese style throughout the weekend and he is none the worse for it.

During this river journey we were thinking how different life is in China, particularly with reference to Sundays. So often the sort of trips, such as we have just made, have to be done over a weekend in order to fit in with the boats and also the amount of time to spare from work. No such thing as half-days in the middle of the week, or shops being shut on Sundays. Our ministers say that they cannot make the Chinese Christians not work on Sundays, as often they would lose their job. Work is not so easily come by for these people.

When we reached home there was a bath waiting for us. The Russell's had thought we should arrive back very hot, dusty and tired after a four-hour, bumpy, truck journey. They had no means of knowing about our good fortune.

On Monday morning I had to start packing our things away for Chaotung and Kuling. We have heard from Chaotung about our house. They are getting one ready for us and we shall have it all to ourselves, also a cook will be waiting for us. I wonder how I shall get along, the dialect is quite a bit different but I believe they understand the Hankow dialect. I expect Frank will add his footnote to this. Winnie

<u>Thursday</u>

Frank:-

It is very unkind of us to have kept you so long without a letter. Our days seem so full and we tire very easily in this weather, so please forgive us. Today we have been to a Garden Party at the British Consulate in honour of the King's birthday.

(This was a cucumber sandwich garden party as mentioned earlier in this narrative.)

<u>June 20th 1948</u> - letter from Hankow.

Frank:-

Mummy's birthday! Many happy returns to you dear. I hope you will have another happy year and keep in good health. We have had a very topsy-turvy week. One boat after another going to Kuling has been commandeered by the Army, and in the end, Winnie and Doris had to go by small riverboat. They with some of the other missionaries went on board on Friday night to leave on Saturday morning. The boat should arrive at Kiu Kiang (nine rivers) today and then they will go by truck to the foot of the hills. The climb up the hill takes two hours. The women and children usually go up by sedan chair and the men walk.

Winnie was sad to leave me behind. How we long for a home of our own and some privacy for a while, but it won't be for long. I'm staying down with Arthur and we hope to go up together (perhaps to fly) in ten days time. Then I shall come down again in August and Winnie in September. The small riverboats are a sight worth seeing. Imagine a tug with an upper deck and some small cabins, cover all the floors, decks and roof with luggage and people sitting packed like sardines in a tin, put a small toilet over the end, then fill the cabins to capacity and you have the picture. The railway trains are just the same - passengers even sit on the train's engine.

The Communists have once again entered one of the small country towns situated one day's journey north of Hankow where we have a hospital and the church. The Chinese doctor and his wife got away a week ago, as they were wanted people. Noel Richards stayed on till Friday and then had to come away as the Communists were giving him no peace. They had carried off six nurses to use in their own hospital behind the lines. The Chinese Minister and Matron are still staying behind and the Matron is running an outpatient department. They are brave people.

KULING - summer 1948 and move to Kunming

June 29th 1948 - letter from Kuling

Winnie:-

We have now been in Kuling for ten days and are expecting Frank and Arthur tomorrow. Since arriving here it has rained incessantly for seven days out of the ten, we are up in the clouds and it just pours down.

The scenery is magnificent. From our bungalow veranda we look right across the valley to the surrounding hills. We are not far from the 'Gap' (the only shopping place) and we are near the favourite walks and beauty spots.

The 'Gap'
Kuling
1948.

The journey from Hankow was most exciting. Our original plan was not possible because the Government for transportation of troops had commandeered all the boats going to Shanghai. We were left high and dry with many other foreigners wanting to get away from the heat. After many weary days of chasing around we ended up buying tickets and cabins on a (hsaio lou lun) small steamer. Between us we bought up all the cabin space, one for eight people, one for four and two for two. These cabins belonged to the crew and the extra money we paid for them went to their respective owners. We had to be on board by eight o'clock on Friday night, 18th. June. Doris and I and the two children shared a two-berth cabin. We had very little room and it was extremely hot. Arthur and Frank came to help us fix up our bedding and other goods and chattels, which Doris considered necessary for the journey. We sprayed the cabins with DDT and sprinkled powder all over the place, in the meantime killing any bedbugs we saw. Arthur and Frank left us about midnight and we tried to settle down for the night. Unfortunately, our torches both failed us so we had to endure the bedbugs in silence. Owing to the small amount of space left for us to sleep, the children were one on each bunk, Doris and I spent a very restless night on the floor.

Before we set sail Arthur Russell had walked around the steamer checking facilities. He returned to us saying,'Under no circumstances venture outside the cabin because there are people with smallpox sitting outside the toilet door.' It was quite a challenge for us to keep two young children closed in the cabin. But there was no chance to move around; the steamer was absolutely jam packed, every inch of deck space being covered with baggage and passengers.

Doris, being a hardened traveller, knew exactly what to do. Whenever either we, or the children, needed to relieve ourselves we used the children's chamber pot. When this became full Doris just called upon one of the passengers parked outside the cabin door, handed them the pot and politely asked them to empty it. Without embarrassment or surprise, the pot was passed from one passenger to the next until it reached the deck railing. Once there the pot was emptied out into the river below and passed back to us with accompanying smiles and nods.

June 29th 1948 - letter continued

Winnie:-

The noise of chattering people, who spread out all over the deck, and loud voiced Army Officers, who kept appearing throughout the night trying to buy cabins at a higher price than we had paid, made for a lively night. Apparently, if the Officers had been fortunate we should just have been tipped out onto the deck.

We set sail at six o'clock in the morning and Doris and I decided to have breakfast. We had tinned salmon (Doris's favourite item of food in the hot season), puffed rice and milk, followed by coffee. After twelve hours sailing we pulled in at Wusueh. Here, we were met by one of our missionaries who invited us to stay the night in the mission compound. After our very bad night on Friday, we four, together with six other ladies, set off. The Captain told us to return by seven o'clock the next morning, as the boat was due to leave at eight. We had a good night's sleep, awoke at five o'clock, had a quick wash and a cup of coffee, rolled up our bedding and hastily walked the three miles or so back to the riverbank, arriving there at six forty-five only to see the steamer sailing off round the bend of the river.

In China there always seems to be some way out. We hired a junk for five million Chinese dollars (about two pounds sterling) and all piled in under the shelter. There was very little wind and the junk gently tacked, criss-cross fashion along the Yangtze, which was pretty wide at this stretch. It took us until two thirty in the afternoon to draw in beside our steamer. Having had no food to eat and nothing to drink since six o'clock in the morning, we hurried to the nearest teashop.

After this we went to the China Travel Service office and were told that all our luggage had gone up the hill, this was a great load off our minds; all we had to do then was get into a lorry to be taken across the plain, and then into a chair and up the hill. What a wonderful sight it was in the sunset! I went up in a chair with little Barbara. Six coolies carried us up, two in front and four behind. The chair bounced terrifically as the men got into stride, a steady swinging motion. Some people are chair-sick, or so they say. I was not. On some corners the angle is so great that the chair is virtually suspended over a huge gap with the front coolies on one side and the back ones on the other.

A coolie path in Kuling.

These coolies must be wonderfully strong. They were skilful at their work. We weren't a bit worried and had complete confidence in them. They continuously climbed the two thousand steps to the top of the hill. After two and a half hours of steady climbing we turned the corner and saw Kuling, a collection of bungalows and some shops nestling on the hillside amongst a lot of trees. During the peak of the season two to three thousand Chinese and foreigners spend their holiday here.

The climate is so damp and humid just now. I washed a few clothes a week ago and they are not yet dry. All our papers, matches, lamps and what have you get wet through. However, the sun does shine and we are praying for a fine day for the men to come up the hill tomorrow. It will take them about three hours. Frank and I are looking forward to a month's holiday to go exploring, before we go back to work. Now I must go to bed, with no electricity it is more economical to go to bed early and get up early.

The bungalows were spacious, each 'flat' being self-contained. There was a large central dining room and sitting area as well as the veranda. Four families usually lived together in one bungalow and the wives were expected to make all provision for catering, turn and turn about. Servants were available to do the actual cooking, washing up and cleaning. I remember being quite apprehensive during my first week of catering for a group of people whom we had only just met. (It was rather like some of our later 1950s holidays in the Nilgiri Hills, India.) I particularly remember that during the torrential monsoon rains it was impossible to hear one another speak because the rain was thundering down so hard upon the corrugated iron roof.

Kuling 'bungalow wives'
Joan Pillow, Winnie and Doris Russell.

After our epic journey from Hankow and late arrival in Kuling, Doris and I hastily unpacked the bedding and made up two beds, gave Martin and little Barbara their supper and put them to bed. After this we settled down for a few minutes to take some refreshment. Taking one look around the bungalow, which had been empty for nine months, Doris and I decided that we were too tired to make up two more beds and dossed down together on the double bed. Doris was quite a buxom lady and at that time I was quite slender. We lay down on the bed and promptly rolled down into the middle. The springs were so slack that it proved to be impossible for us to remain apart, so in the end I slept on the floor and Doris remained in the bed. A few days later we were joined by two other families and settled down to enjoy a very happy holiday, with good company and plenty of activities.

Kuling
as seen from
the plains.

<u>Sunday July 4th 1948</u> - letter from Kuling.

Frank:-

At last we have arrived in Kuling, I do wish you were here to see what sort of place it is. Mummy and Daddy would find it quite equal to all their dreams of Switzerland and John would have all the mountains to climb that he could desire. We are living in a little bungalow in a valley on top of the mountain. The bungalow is divided into four flats with a common dining room and sitting room. Our little flat has a bedroom, a study and a bathroom. From our window we have a wonderful view of the valley. A long veranda runs the length of the front of the house and we can sit there to rest, eat and read.

Arthur and I arrived here on Thursday. We went on board the 'An Kong', one of the biggest riverboats, on Wednesday evening at about nine o'clock. We were travelling saloon class - a class even higher than first class - yet the fare was only seven shillings and six pence. We had very comfortable armchairs on a part of the deck kept free for saloon passengers, and spent quite a pleasant night. The ship left at about two o'clock in the night and we made a very rapid journey down the river arriving at Kuling at two o'clock on Thursday afternoon. What a contrast to Winnie's uncomfortable, two-day journey in a small boat!

The English Vice-Consul and his wife were on our boat and they had arranged for a truck to meet them and take their baggage to the bottom of the hill. They invited us to share the truck with them. Arthur and I then did the climb to the top of the hill. We took about three hours over it because our baggage coolies were tired and consequently slow.

The climb was very beautiful, along a twisting path with hundreds of steps and teahouses along the way. Here and there were streams where the coolies were able to wash. We are now three thousand five hundred feet up and sometimes look down on the clouds, indeed occasionally, we are in the middle of them. There are many walks in all directions. Two to three thousand foreigners will be up here this summer. There are two churches, a Union Church and an Anglican one. Already they are packed with people. Winnie has joined the choir.

Near our bungalow is a little gorge with a stream and bathing pool. There is a small paddling pool for the children, which needs cleaning. There is a very large community swimming pool as well.

Behind us rises one of the ridges of the mountain, which, at its highest, is four thousand five hundred feet. Hankow is now very hot and sticky and the air here is so cool and refreshing. Winnie will be staying up for August as well, but I will be going down to take over the eye department for Dr. Cundall.

A Bungalow group in Kuling 1948.

<u>Sunday July 11th 1948</u> - letter from Kuling.

Frank:-

Sunday has come again, and it is hard to think that more than a week has gone by in this beautiful countryside. The mountains form a group about ten miles long and five miles wide, and from any point on the circumference, there are wonderful views over the plain with its hundreds of small lakes and the huge Poyang Lake. You can see the brown, muddy, Yangtze, threading its way between the blue coloured lakes. As the streams leave the mountains and cross the plain, one can see widening rows and rows of rice fields.

The Yangtze in flood snaking across the plain

Frank continued:-

This is a pottery area and on one side are white kaolin quarries. One can buy very beautiful chinaware and Winnie has bought a set of rice bowls for Chaotung. They also do very fine embroidery work. At the moment, the prices are too high, but we hope they will fall in proportion when our exchange rises.

This week we had the weekly prayer meeting in our bungalow and already we form quite a large Methodist gathering. The recent arrivals have had to travel rather uncomfortably in small river steamers (Hsiao Ho Lun - small fire wheel). The troops have again commandeered the larger boats. The aeroplanes have been withdrawn because of petrol shortage, and there is no airmail direct to Kuling now. This morning the large Union Church was packed full and by no means all the holidaymakers have arrived. The choir sang a very beautiful anthem. Winnie is glad to be able to join a choir once again. Every Sunday night we go to the house of one of the retired missionaries living in Kuling and sing hymns.

Arthur Russell looking out over Poyang Lake.

Arthur and I have been for two long walks, and Winnie and I have been for shorter ones. Yesterday, we formed a large party and went for an all day hike. We started by going to a cave in the face of the hill called 'The Cave of the Immortals' or 'Fairies'. There was a breathtaking view through the clouds on to the plain three thousand feet or more below. In the cave was a spring of holy water and an Idol, tended by Taoist priests. The priests have their hair long and coiled into a bun on top, transfixed by a wooden pin. Nearby were two pavilions or 'tin sen' (little shelters on rocky promontories), from which there were wonderful views. One of the temples was erected in memory of a General who won his battles by following the advice of a madman.

We then descended into the main valley of the range and followed a stream to the ruins of some incense mills. Here was a large pool where some of us bathed, while the rest lit a fire and brewed some tea. After lunch, a party of four of us did some stiff climbing to the bottom of the waterfall where the stream plunges three hundred feet down the hill.

A 'tin-sen'.

We had a hot and strenuous climb back up again, had another bathe and tea and then started our walk back through the woods on the other side of the stream. On our way we stopped for more tea (it was such a hot day) at a Buddhist Temple of the Yellow Dragon. A large yellow stone set in the floor of the temple represents the yellow dragon's head. The monks started to chant their evening prayers as we drank the tea. They asked for no money, and we gave them gifts for their hospitality. After supper we had some friends in for a party and played games together.

Already we are feeling much better for the holiday. Winnie has found time to do some painting, and I am reading some fiction and books about China. The swimming pools are nearly ready so we shall soon have bathing near at hand.

We are quite near Chiang Kai-Chek's summerhouse. It is being prepared for his arrival, arranging flower gardens and tidying the roads. Their house seems very carefully guarded, but has large and beautiful gardens.

Sunday 18th July 1948 - letter from Kuling.

Frank:-

The beginning of this week was quite rainy and this prevented us from going on any very long excursions. On Monday afternoon we set out, with our tea, during what seemed to be a fine spell. We were hoping to find 'Dragon's Pool', a place where two streams meet. We were soon caught in the rain. The paths were very overgrown and through woods, they soon became small torrents. The main streams were a marvellous sight, being greatly swollen, rushing down the steep hillside from rock to rock.

On our return journey we took a detour because one path was flooded, and then we found the alternative path also under water. So we took off our shoes and socks and paddled. Soon the sun came out again and dried us. The mountain storms are terrific and one is soaked through in a very little time.

Another day Winnie and I climbed to the second highest point on the mountains, the Poyang Ridge, at four thousand and six feet. From this point we could see all the way round, with the Yangtze on the North side and the Poyang Lake to the South.

We then descended about two thousand feet to see the 'Three Waterfalls'. At this point we were in cloud and we had only one short glimpse of the falls when the cloud lifted. These mountain paths are, in many places, old temple paths or coolie tracks.

Winnie at 'The Three Graces' waterfall.

On our way back we climbed one thousand six hundred and eighty five steps and there were many more to go down in addition to those going upwards.

One day this week we spent cleaning out the bathing pool. The bottom was full of sand and stones. The pool is just by the side of the compound, very convenient for a quick bathe.

Last night we had a moonlight picnic to celebrate Doris Russell's birthday. We walked to the 'Cave of the Immortals' and sat in a shelter overlooking the plain. The priests at the temple boiled the kettle for us to make tea. Much of the plain is now flooded. The town of Kiukiang (nine rivers) at which the riverboats call for Kuling, is underwater, and now it is difficult for passengers to get up and down from the foot of the hill. We have taken a few photographs, but the expense of films prevents us from taking many.

Sunday July 25th 1948 - letter written in Kuling and posted in Hankow.

Frank:-

This week we had two big day excursions. One day Winnie and I went to a rocky prominence called 'Dragon's Tooth'. There we found a stone shelter. A staircase wound up the outside and onto the flat roof on which stood a stone table and four seats. From it we could see the top of a long waterfall down the 'Devil's Wall', and on one side miles over the Yangtze plain and on the other, the village of Kuling. From time to time the clouds would blow over and obscure the view. We spent the afternoon looking at the scenery with the binoculars and Winnie sketched the waterfall. I had brought the camera with me but, unfortunately, no spool to wind the film on, so we were not able to take any photos. The walk was a very pleasant one through woods.

On Friday, I had a more strenuous walk. Arthur and I joined an LMS missionary, called Bagley, to make a day trip down to the plain. We started soon after seven o'clock and climbed to the top of the mountain and descended the other side. We went down a steep gorge curving below a series of five towering crags called 'The Lions Leap'. We got down to the foothills by about ten o'clock and the path wound over them to a Buddhist Monastery called 'High Way'. We entered one of the courts by a side entrance and found it full of soldiers. They had come about two days before and were part of the protection in readiness for the Generalissimo, Chiang Kai-Chek.

(Information from Wikipedia:- Chiang Kai-Chek led the Northern Expedition in 1928, unifying China and becoming China's overall leader, the 'Generalissimo'. In 1948 he was still serving as Chairman of the National Military Council of the Nationalist Government of the Republic of China. The Communist uprising started in 1948 and later forced the Nationalist Government retreat to Taiwan, where Chiang Kai-Chek ruled with an iron fist, as 'President of the Republic of China' and 'Director General of the Kuomintang', until his death in 1975.)

Sunday July 25th 1948 - letter continued.

Frank:-

We explored several of the courtyards and temples and eventually met a man dressed very simply in black. We thought him to be a temple servant. He called us to follow him and led us into the guest room. We were given tea, ginger, bamboo shoots, peanuts, melon seeds and pears, and sat down and chatted to him. He turned out to be the Chief Priest. One or two other monks came in and joined us, the Chief Priest then went and fetched two books for us to see. One was part of the Buddhist classics written in gold on a black paper with some fine line drawings. Another was one of eighty books written from the classics in blood. A monk had daily taken some of his own blood and mixed it with an equal amount of water and used this to write with. Eventually he died of anaemia.

The Japanese had destroyed fifty of their books. The monks gave us an invitation to come and stay when we pleased and followed us to the gate as we left. Would you anywhere get such a welcome in an English church if you were a Chinese?

As we left the monastery we passed through the ruins of a large Military Academy, once Chiang Kai-Chek's pride, but bombed, until it was flat, by the Japs. We then wandered along the main road, (this would be a cart track in England) passed kaolin pits, and then took a path through fields to a ruined monastery and Confucian University called 'White Deer Grotto' (Ber Low Doung). A Chinese scholar, 'Jew Shi', had founded the monastery in 800 AD. After the revolution, it was an agricultural college, but the Japs then greatly damaged it, and it has been uninhabited ever since. The courtyards and rooms are in a bad state of ruin, but there are many Confucian tablets still on the walls.

Behind the temple was a small cave with a tablet and stone image of a white deer. The founder 'Jew Shi' had a tame white deer, which followed him like Mary's lamb. A courteous Chinese gentleman was there, making rubbings of the tablets to sell to visitors. He was selling them at a ridiculously low sum. I bought four for Winnie. Two of his sons came by and he asked them to give us some tea as we passed through their village.

The Li family village was made up of members of his family. All had the same surname because girls were married out into other villages. They had lived here for four hundred years, and knew exactly where their ancestors came from on the other side of the Province. We were invited in and given tea to drink - a very weak, boiling hot tea with no milk or sugar. We drank cups and cups of tea and gossiped about their family, and in turn, they asked our name, how old we were and how many children we had, and so on. Everybody you meet in China asks these things and going along the road in the country you ask most passers-by where they are going and if they have eaten.

We left the Li family and went on to the 'Goddess of Mercy Bridge'. It crosses a small gorge in a wonderfully constructed single span of five rows of interlocking stones. Here we met three of the younger women missionaries who had come down a more direct way. We bathed in two deep pools, had tea, visited the temple and took photographs. Then, at about 6.30 we started the journey back. We walked through flooded rice fields and villages for about an hour. The rice looks green at this time of year, and irrigation channels and streams flood all the fields.

We then started to climb the mountain. There were three thousand five hundred steps to be climbed and it grew dark as we climbed, a thunderstorm arrived, with flashes of lightning all around the hills. We went on by torchlight, stopping for tea at a wayside teahouse. At the top (ten-thirty pm) we had supper, and then we walked on, arriving home at eleven forty-five. Winnie and Doris were waiting for us with hot baths ready, and we soon got to bed.

July 27th 1948 - letter written in Kuling continued.

Frank:-

Today we have spent packing and seeing friends. Tomorrow I go down the hill and hope to get the boat the same day. There are supposed to be three calling at Kuling so we should find room on one. Yesterday Winnie and I had a very happy day at the 'Dragon's Pool' only a little way from here. We had the pool to ourselves and spent the whole day there. The weather today has become extremely hot and I'm glad Winnie will not have to go down to the plain for a while.

'Paradise'
one of the beautiful
waterfalls of Kuling.

August 1st August 1948 - letter from Hankow to Frank's brother, John.

Frank:-

Outside the window someone has just been banging cymbals and a drum. Chinese music to our ears is an awful discord. They blow whistles, bang drums, cymbals and triangles, seemingly out of time, and thoroughly enjoy it. This type of music is especially associated with Buddhist ceremonies, and when we hear it, it usually means a funeral or wedding, or that a boat is just setting off on a long journey and is seeking the blessings of the gods.

H. B. Rattenbury's book, 'My China, My China', gives you a very good description of this part of China and the life of the people. He describes Hankow and the Methodist General Hospital.

You would laugh to see me now, it is dark and I am sitting in our study. Little wall lizards are running over the outside of the mosquito net. Arthur is downstairs alternately tuning in the wireless and typing a letter. I am wearing just sandals and shorts and oozing sweat all over which keeps trickling down my back. From time to time I try to dry off with a fan and then write a little more. We sleep at night on a straw mat covered by a sheet lying on top of the mattress. There are still a few mosquitoes around so I have kept up our mosquito net.

Arthur and I left Kuling (and our wives) on Wednesday last. We had a very comfortable journey. Kuikiang, the port at the bottom of the hill, was flooded and we had to paddle around carrying our shoes and socks in our hands. We managed to get on a large riverboat in the evening. These boats have five classes: saloon, first, second, third and deck passengers. The saloon class is the one we most use because, in the heat, it is the only one reasonably comfortable. These boats are terribly crowded and it is very easy to pick up infections in this hot weather. However, this time there were no tickets available, so we bought deck passenger tickets and then slept on the floor in the saloon class corridor and used their lounge and bought the saloon class food. It was very comfortable and we were in Hankow by three o'clock on Thursday afternoon. Compare this with four days or so it would take in a small boat of the type Winnie travelled on. I do hope she has as comfortable a journey as we had this time.

Arthur has temporarily taken over the work of Medical Superintendent here. I am doing the eye work while Dr Cundall is away, mostly trachoma, interstitial keratitis and corneal ulcers. Next week, a patient is coming in with an anterior dislocation of the lens and I'm wondering if I should take the lens out or wait for Dr. Cundall's return from holiday.

One afternoon a week I am going to try being on emergency call and see how I can cope with the language problem. Arthur will be the second on call so he will be able to come to my rescue. We are quite a small establishment of four 'bachelors' now in Hankow. We feed together in one house but still live in our own houses.

The Yangtze Valley has been badly flooded, but so far, the dykes at Hankow have held. There was a disastrous flood here in 1931, and the water has been almost as high again this year. New dykes were built some years ago and they have kept the water back but above and below Hankow, there is bad flooding.

The political situation here is still chaotic. The Government is crippled by the civil war and seems to us terribly incompetent and corrupt. The Communists make steady progress and prices continue to soar and soar. Europe seems far away to us, but the news is sinister. Somehow it seems we have to learn to live with Communism. It has come to a stage in political evolution to stay. We know that what is bad in it cannot last because of the nature of right and wrong in God's world. What seems so important is that Christians should always be in the heart of the situation making their contribution, knowing that in some way God is bringing his Kingdom, though at times it is impossible for us to know how He is doing it. Please give everybody our love.

<u>August 7th 1948</u> - letter from Kuling.

Winnie:-

Many apologies for the lapse of a week in writing, but many things have been happening up here on the hill. On Wednesday, July 28th, Frank went back to Hankow. I went part of the way down the hill with him and then returned. These times of parting seem rather hard. One feels only half in one place and half in the other - the best half is missing, if you know what I mean. On the other hand they are good in that, through letters, one often gets to know the other better.

Thursday evening I had dinner with the Hawthorn's, and yesterday it was Kit Cundall's wedding, a really happy day for everyone. The service was led by Mr Heady and brought back happy memories because they had the same scripture reading as us and one of the hymns was the same. The church was beautifully decorated with huge white lilies, which grow wild on the hillside. Doris and I made Kit's bridal hat. Our household was responsible for making the biscuits and some cakes for the reception, and also for looking after the children. I helped Doris Russell with these and yesterday set the tables, arranged flowers, made jellies, lemonade etc. Quite a busy time altogether, love Winnie.

August 15th 1948 - letter written in Kuling and posted in Hankow.

Winnie:-

All this past week I have been practising with the other British Methodists for a concert to be given on Monday 16th. It's great fun and good relaxation but takes quite a lot of time off language study for those of us who are plodding along. I am to dress up as the 'New Look'. I have made myself a hat out of paper, taking the pattern from somebody's fashion book. I do look the shoot! I hope the 'new look' has not come to stay, if so we shall really look old-fashioned when we come home.

We also put on a performance of part of Oscar Wilde's play, 'The Importance of being Earnest'.

On Thursday, the Generalissimo and Madame Chiang Kai-Chek arrived in Kuling and they were both at church this morning. The church was absolutely packed, with men sitting on the windowsills and anywhere else they could find. We have had news that we are to leave for Hankow on September the 20th approximately, so I shall be going down the hill at the end of this month, when we shall pack our bags and go on our way. Poor old Frank will be alone for his birthday unless there is a party going down the hill the previous week. We ladies are not allowed to travel with baggage by ourselves. The coolies would simply nobble us with their high prices realising that, if we refuse to pay their price, we could not carry the things ourselves.

Sunday August 15th 1948 - letter from Hankow.

Frank:-

This week hospital life has gone on much as I have described before. We have all been kept fairly busy, some of the doctors have been on holiday and some ill, the hot weather brings quite a lot of diseases. Arthur has quite a lot to do deputising as Medical Superintendent. The money problem is one of the big ones. The hospital is self-supporting, apart from the missionary doctors' and nurses' salaries, which the Mission pays. For the first ten days of each month all the income is spent on buying supplies, drugs, bedding, firewood etc. For the rest of the month it is stored in the safe for paying salaries. The trouble is that it so quickly loses its value unless the illegal silver dollars are bought. A new issue of five million dollar notes has just come out, and this always means a bigger jump in exchange. The official rate of exchange has just jumped from fifteen million to twenty two million C.N.C. (Chinese National Currency Dollars) to one pound sterling, and the unofficial rate is about fifty per cent higher. The silver dollar on Thursday was worth four and a half million C.N.C. and now has gone up to five and a half million C.N.C., so it is quite a worry for Arthur to keep track of it.

In the hospital the doctors have to act as almoners, charging the patients for everything as it is needed, be it drugs, operation fees, x-ray charges, bandages and other such commodities, and we have to keep an eye on the rising prices.

This week and the coming week the Chinese have the Festival for the Departed Spirits. In a narrow road between our houses and the hospital one can see the Chinese burning paper money, and leaving pieces of cash, gold and silver, and little sticks of incense for the spirits to use in the other world. If they are more wealthy they burn little paper models of houses, rickshaws and servants; all that the spirits will need for their comfort in the other world. At night on the river, they float down lighted coloured paper lanterns to comfort the souls of those who have been drowned. Last night Arthur and I had walked over to the Union Hospital and on our way back we saw a stall covered with a canvas awning. On either side were paper images, some three feet high, and other smaller gods in little temples and houses. At either end was an altar with lighted candles. Around one sat Buddhist monks with drums, triangles and cymbals. One monk stood in front, chanting and waving a stick with strings of coloured paper on the end and, in between his chanting, the orchestra played.

During this hot weather everyone sleeps out of doors and people come out and sit in the teashops and drink tea until after midnight. At several places stages have been erected ready for performances of some old Chinese plays, which seem to go on and on forever. In many of the teashops storytellers sit and large crowds gather round to hear the stories.

Today has been cloudy and we have had a breeze and some showers, the temperature has dropped. It has been 88° to 100°F in the shade and the air is almost saturated because of the river nearby (75 per cent humidity) so today's coolness has been very welcome.

August 22nd 1948 - extracts from a letter from Hankow.

Frank:-

This week I visited the Air Transport Officer again and it seems that we shall be able to get a plane after all from Hankow to Kunming on

September 20th. This will be much better for us than going by train first to Canton, which was the alternative.

The Government has made a desperate effort to stop the inflation by issuing new currency now, in dollars. It is going to be backed by gold (so they say) and will keep its value. If so, the exchange may be in our favour. At the moment our day-to-day cost of living has been two-thirds to three-quarters our stipend and now it will be only a half. If the dollar maintains its value we may be able to save some money instead of having to spend it before it loses its value. The change in currency has meant that we have all gone without money in Hankow for two weeks now. The banks have none so I've not been able to get the photos printed for Mummy. We have had all we've needed in a way of food but nothing to spare. Winnie, on the other hand, has been able to get some money in Kuling and has thirty-two silver dollars to spare. Such is China. Either way, please don't feel anxious about food. Our standard of living is much, much better than at home, with eggs at one penny each, and so on.

September 6th 1948 - letter from Hankow.

Winnie:-

Soon our address will be Chaotung. I returned to Hankow on Sunday, my journey from Kuling had its excitement, as do all such journeys in China. Five of us had booked cabins on a boat for the 3rd of September, and later were told that there was no room and the boat would be two days late. We decided to ring the China Travel Service at the bottom of the hill and were told another large boat would be leaving Kiukiang at eight o'clock on Thursday evening, so we hurriedly packed our bags and went. It took us one and a half hours to walk down the hill. We three 'girls' only had five minutes rest, despite the fact that our legs felt a little weak after going down the two thousand steps.

When we reached the bottom of the hill we piled, luggage and all, into a truck and went across the plain to the China Travel Service Office, only to be told, the boat would not be in until the next day. So we had a meal and found a Chinese Inn for the night. The Inn was a good one, with clean beds and plenty of water for drinking and washing. Mr Heady spent Friday and Saturday mornings going from one shipping office to another and we eventually got tickets for the Kiang Lin and went on board at six o'clock on Saturday evening.

The Kiang Lin was a beautiful boat, fitted with electric fans, a lounge, a good dining-room and cabins on the first class deck, where we were supposed to be. Below were other travel classes. It was a terrific scramble to get on board at all and we had to enter on the bottom deck and work our way up through the inside. There were just masses of people, at every step we trod on bundles or feet and it was stifling hot. How those poor people endured it I cannot imagine. We heard afterwards that two previous large boats had been commandeered by the troops, hence the congestion. We were given a small Chinese meal for our supper and slept, some on the dining room chairs, some on the floor and others on the tables. At eight o'clock on Sunday morning we were in Hankow and I gave Frank a surprise by arriving home unexpectedly at ten thirty. He was told we should not arrive until Monday.

In my letter I did not mention the fact that Kiukiang was flooded and we waded everywhere in two to three feet of swirling, muddy water, with our arms linked as a safeguard against falling into the huge, open, sewage drains that ran between the pavements and roadways throughout the town. The river had risen quite a lot since Frank and Arthur's departure.

Immediately, on my return to Hankow from Kunming, I began packing our belongings, ready for the journey to Chaotung, while Frank was fully occupied chasing up the transport arrangements for our journey.

As I mentioned earlier, our knowledge of China was quite limited when we first set off from England. During the voyage out we both read the two books recommended by Mission House but, once in Hankow, what with language study and hospital work, as well as adapting to a completely new way of life, we thought no more about preparation for our move to Chaotung. We just knew that it was 'quite remote'.

At first it had been thought that for the initial stage of our journey to Chaotung, we would travel by train to Canton and, from there, take a flight to Kunming. However, word came that the Chinese Airways were starting a direct air service from Hankow to Kunming. Their first plane was going out on September 20th and, better still, it was half-empty and would take an unlimited quantity of luggage. As we were to travel with extra packing cases containing some goods for the Chaotung Hospital, this arrangement was ideal and we gratefully accepted the offer. At long last we were going to reach the end of our journey, where we could settle down in a home of our own for four or five years. So it was that we embarked upon our very first flight on September 20th 1948.

September 22nd 1948 - letter sent from the Methodist Church, Kunming.

Frank:-

The plane was luxuriously furnished. We were served a picnic lunch and a cup of tea in the afternoon. We flew over vast floods in Hunan and the mountains of Kweichow. At times we were above the clouds and could see nothing, then the clouds would clear and we could see for miles around. The plane flew at twelve thousand feet and it became quite cold.

Y U N N A N - 1948 to 1949

Monday September 27th 1948 - letter from Kunming.

Frank:-

We are still in Kunming and have had an exciting and hectic week getting ready to go to Chaotung. Our departure has had to be postponed three times and now we hope to leave on Wednesday. Winnie has bought some stores. I have been able to meet quite a number of the doctors in Kunming and made some very useful contacts. We have attended two feasts given by the local doctors, one arranged especially in our honour.

Out on Kunming Lake with friends.
Keith Parsons faces the camera in the photo above.

On Saturday we had a delightful day's outing over the Kunming Lake (West Lake) to the house of 'Uncle' Evans, the supernumerary who lives here. We had Chinese lunch with him and then climbed to see one of the world famous temples on the Western Hills. Auntie Irene has pictures of them in her National Geographic Magazine.

Sunday October 10th 1948 - letter from the Methodist Hospital, Chaotung.

Frank:-

We arrived in Kunming on 20th September as originally intended. Kenneth Parsons arrived two days later with a station wagon from Chaotung. We had anticipated having to travel without our luggage so he had not brought the truck. The station wagon needed repairs and registration, so we did not get away from Kunming until 29th September. Whilst there we found a shop where they made harmoniums and Winnie had one especially made for her birthday. It folds up and is fitted with a strap handle to make it easily transportable. Winnie is delighted with it. She has already become church organist and is going to help with the music at the club.

Ken Grant, the business manager of the Church Missionary Society's Hospital is an old Friends' Ambulance Unit man. He is going to keep us up to date with salary scales and drug prices. There is a very experienced American surgeon there who was Professor of Surgery in Philadelphia and, on retiring, came to China at his own expense for two to three years to do some teaching. On Sunday morning we had a very helpful ward round together.

We finally set off from Kunming on Wednesday, 29th September, with Ken Parsons driving the station wagon. We left six packing cases behind to come on later and packed the rest of the luggage into the station wagon and trailer. The first part of the journey was fairly flat. The road was mud and stone but in good condition, much better than the roads in Hupeh. We had only one breakdown that day when one of the leads of the coil burnt through.

At this point I think it a good time to give some information about our new surroundings. The Province of Yunnan was such a huge contrast from Hankow city, with its huge, noisy, teeming people rushing about in the busy market. On our journey from Kunming to Chaotung, we drove for mile after mile without meeting another human being. The villages were far apart and very small. Most villages were surrounded by high walls, and secured with heavy gates that were locked after dark. Bandits roamed around at will and were likely to attack travellers in isolated places and rob them of all their money. Often their clothing was taken as well. From time to time a village would be plundered and all livestock and other valuables stolen.

The original inhabitants of this region were the Nosu tribe, who were wealthy landowners, rather like Feudal Barons, and their serfs, the Miao people, who tilled their land and were very poor. Over the centuries, the Han Chinese had fled into Yunnan during times of unrest, to settle and build walled cities, which were defended by soldiers, with the city gates locked at night. Chaotung was one such city.

Szu Szu U Hu
Yunnan Province

When travelling across this almost barren land on that first journey, we were struck by the immense vastness and grandeur of the mountains. It gave us time to think and ponder, following the upheaval of the previous six months of our lives. I wonder now, were we at all apprehensive as to what might follow? I cannot say, because, in a strange kind of way, to us this was an exciting adventure into the unknown.

Typical Yunnan country.

Sunday October 10th 1948 - letter continued.

Frank:-

At about four o'clock we arrived at a Chinese Inn situated just outside a village. Imagine a small, whitewashed building with a heavy wooden door and piles of barley stooks at the entrance. Inside, one entered a courtyard of mud with an open drain running round and water tubs towards one side. On two sides of the courtyard were rooms with wooden walls going halfway up. On the third side were open stables for the horses, cows and pigs. On the fourth side were storerooms. Upstairs a veranda ran around the courtyard and crude wooden walls were put up to make a rough room here and there. The windows were holes in the wall with wooden shutters. There was a polished wood round table where we ate a very nice supper of rice, eggs, bacon and vegetables.

The smoke from the kitchen below floated up through the floor and found its way out through the roof. All the wastewater was just thrown overboard into the courtyard below, making sure no one was in the way. As Chinese Inn's go it was a very clean and comfortable one. We put down our camp beds and slept well, getting up just before dawn to have breakfast 'on the road'.

As Frank said, we spent a reasonably comfortable night. This was largely because we were able to sleep on our own camp beds in our own bedding, having liberally sprinkled DDT powder on the floor all around each camp bed leg to ward off the bed bugs.

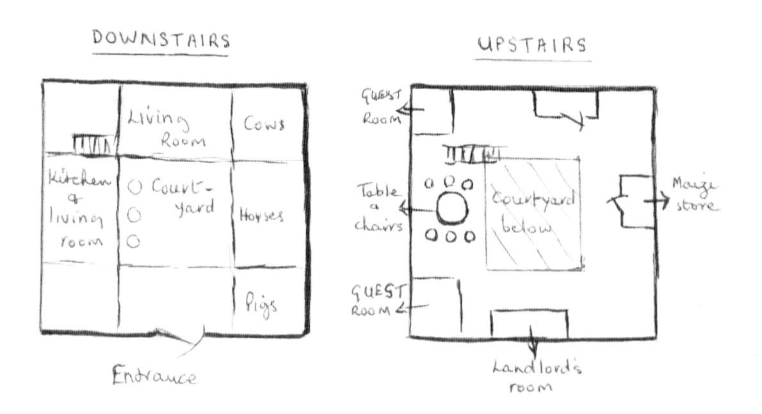

Layout of the Chinese inn.

Up to this point we had travelled along the end of the Burma Road, built during the Second World War, and this was relatively smooth. After leaving the inn, the condition of the road gradually deteriorated. Very soon we were crashing through huge potholes and negotiating our way passed large rock boulders, which threatened to block our path, until, at last, we were defeated.

<u>Sunday October 10th 1948</u> - letter continued.

Frank:-

The second day was quite eventful. Alas, the trailer was too heavy for the car and at about nine o'clock the towing girder on the station wagon snapped in half. We turned round and made our way back to Shanwei, a small, walled country town. Outside the town was a lorry depot and we drove in there. They were most kind to us. They found a length of steel and got it drilled so that it could be screwed onto our towing girder. We lightened the trailer by taking off three of our boxes to come on by lorry later. We were given a simple lunch of rice, eggs and tomatoes and set off again at about one thirty.

The rest of the day's journey was over mountains, the road wound in and out, often turning back on itself as we climbed. The scenery was spectacular. As we came down the other side of the mountains darkness fell. We arrived in Weining, nine thousand feet above sea level, at about eight o'clock. We stayed there the night with Elliott and Ruth Kendall.

At Weining we left a little more luggage to lighten the load and picked up a Chinese schoolmaster's wife who was coming to the hospital to have her baby. The road from then on became awful. Imagine the worst possible farmhouse track with patches of mud, great potholes and ruts, in places large boulders, and in other places a terrific camber so that the differential touches the road. This road climbs up and down the mountains with, in places, steep drops on one side and rock on the other. At one point there was a deep river to cross. This day our petrol pump began to fail. The car stopped on every steep hill when we changed into bottom gear because it wasn't getting any petrol. Finally, it gave out altogether on a hill twenty-five li (three li equals one mile) from Chaotung.

Kenneth decided to spend the night in the car and we started to walk into Chaotung with the intention of sending the truck out to meet Kenneth next morning. Poor Mrs Li, the schoolmaster's wife, was making bad progress, and it looked as if Winnie and she would have to spend the night in a farmhouse - not to be desired. Then, by a stroke of providence, along came a Hwa Gan, a light carrying chair, one could go the days without seeing one. We hired this and put Mrs Li in it and set off at a good pace.

A Hwa Gan (carrying litter)

Actually, Mrs Li did not ride all the way because, with typical Chinese courtesy, she insisted that I rode for a while first. This I did, but not for long, because the motion of the bamboo poles swinging up and down as the coolies jogged along was most uncomfortable. As we walked along, Frank was giving me instructions as to the intricacies of preparing for delivery of a baby in a village hut miles from any assistance. Eventually, we arrived in Chaotung between eight and nine o'clock in pitch darkness. Thankfully, Mrs Li did use the chair and we escorted her safely to the Maternity Ward where she gave birth to a lovely baby the following day.

Everyone on the Mission Compound assumed we should not be arriving until the next morning and had gone to bed. We banged on the entrance gate and after much shouting, accompanied by ferocious barking of dogs, the gate was opened and we were escorted through the compound by the light of a single hurricane lamp. The guard dogs were kept chained all day and then let loose during the hours of darkness. They were quite vicious and kept darting out from behind the hedges to snap at the backs of our legs. It was a rather tense and frightening five minutes. Of course, as a result of all the noise and commotion our colleagues arose from their beds and gave us a tremendous welcome. After some drink and refreshment we were shown to our beds.

Sunday October 10th 1948 - letter continued.

Frank:-

That night, we stayed with the Thexton's. Leslie Thexton is the Chairman of the District. Next morning as we were getting the truck ready to go out to meet Kenneth, in he came with the station wagon. He had put some wire round the petrol pump plunger to make it fit and then tied a petrol tin high above the bonnet.

Letter continued Monday October 11th

Frank:-

Chaotung is a small, walled city. The hospital is on a hill about half a mile outside the East Gate. This hill is made of clay and is constantly moving. In consequence, all the buildings are gradually falling apart. Last year one house fell down; the end walls of our house are falling outwards and sinking so that there are large gaps in the wall and the French windows have to be refitted once a month. We are very thrilled with a house of our own nonetheless.

Our boxes being carried into the gate of the Chaotung Hospital house courtyard.

Yesterday, we moved in properly. Until then we were staying with the Thexton's. The length of the house runs from North to South.

The North side is very cold because of the prevailing winds

The front door is at the South side of the house.

Inside is a small waiting room with Chinese type chairs and tables for Chinese guests. This opens into the passageway. Our study is a large room near the front door with massive bookshelves and a long desk. The middle room has sliding wooden partitions on two sides. We are planning to make it a spare bedroom. The dining room is next to the kitchen. The kitchen has a small stove and is nicely equipped with table and cupboards. Before long a sink is supposed to be coming.

We have three servants in the house, the cook, a boy who carries water, lights the fires and washes up, and a woman who does the washing and housecleaning.

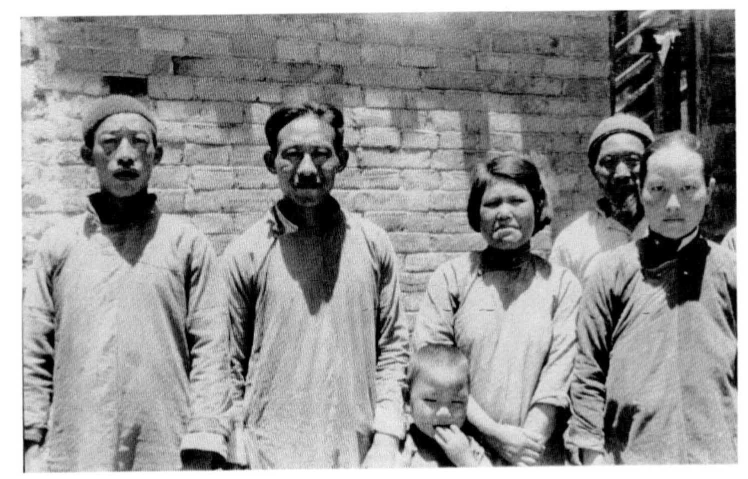

Left to right: Lungtse, cook, cook's wife and son, the water carrier and housemaid.

There is a very nice garden, where the flowers are profuse. We have a deaf gardener, called 'Lungtse' and brother to the cook, who comes in once a week.

Lungtse and our mongrel puppy 'Sally'.

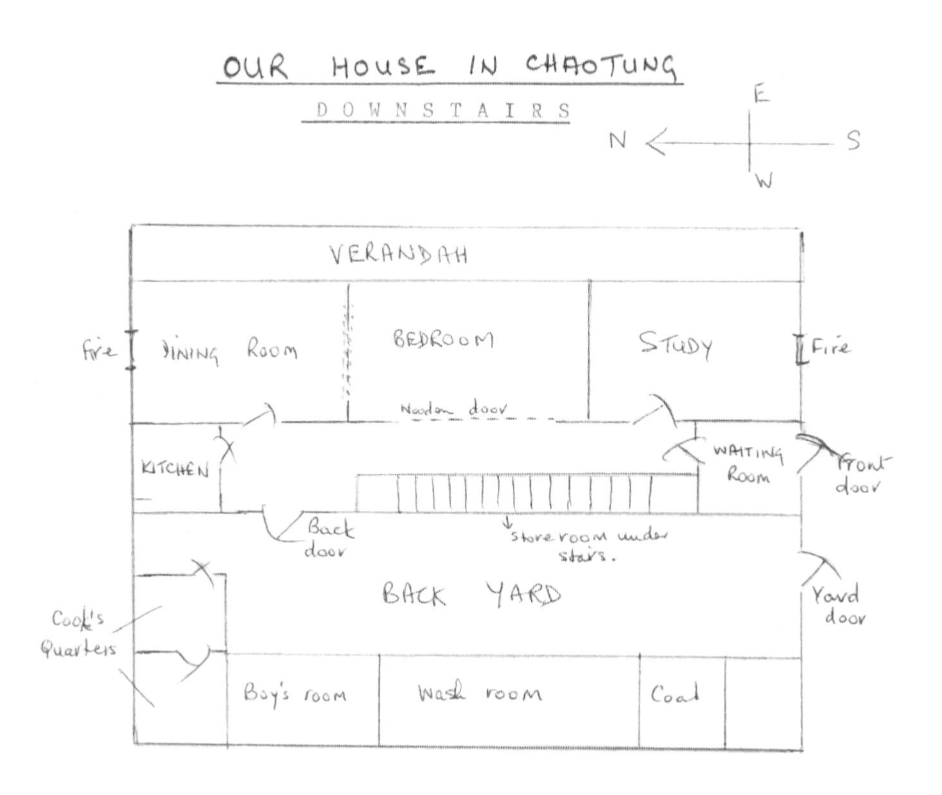

Upstairs on the south side is our sitting room and in the middle is our bedroom. Dr Galbraith has the north room as her sitting room and a little bedroom opening off.

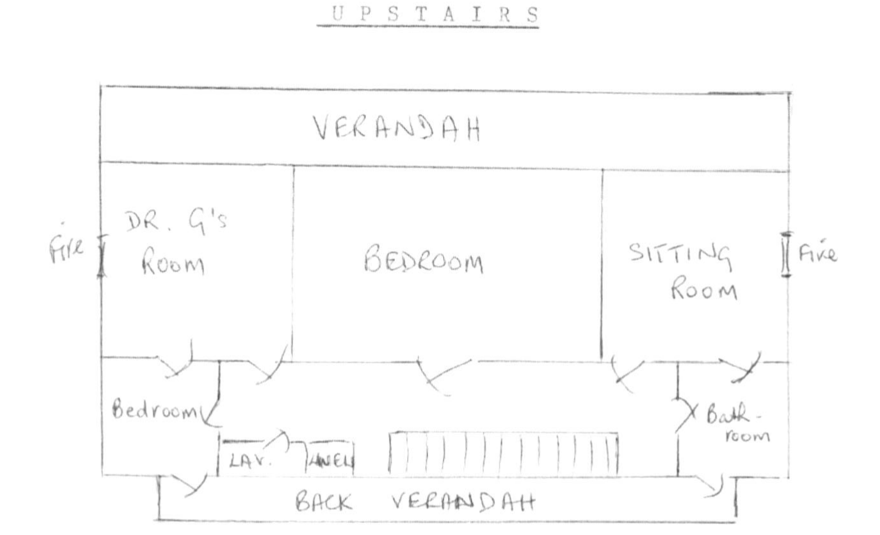

From our windows we have a marvellous panoramic view across the plain to the rows of mountains beyond. The farmers have just been getting in the maize harvest and the fields are golden with regular rows of stooks.

The hospital is just outside the garden gate. I must tell you more about it next time I write. This week I have been getting to know what instruments are there and looking through the stores. In the stores are lots of new instruments. The x-ray machine and generator were still packed up and we have to set them up.

The last three days have been quite eventful because we've had a succession of earthquakes, two large ones and many small ones. Quite a lot of damage has been done in the City and the missionaries have come out to stay on the hospital compound. There have been quite a few casualties. Our own house has cracked more and part of the roof has fallen off. Here's another tremor, just now!

And now for some special news! We are expecting a baby about April next year. Winnie wants me to tell you that she has almost everything she will need. We both feel so happy about this news and are so glad that all our travelling has ended safely.

October 17th October 1948 - letter from Chaotung.

Frank:-

I'm sitting on one side of the fire - our own fire at last - and Winnie is by my side writing to her people at Bedford. In front, on the hearthrug, are our two cats. One is a Siamese, a handsome gentleman called 'Sebastian', and the other is a little lady, still very young and kittenish, called 'Sweetheart'. They were given to us by the Stone family, who have just left for Hong Kong, and they were already named when we arrived. At first they disappeared up the chimney in fright and stayed there for four whole days until hunger forced them down.

Letter continued October 19th

Frank:-

Since starting this letter we've had two of your letters arrive from home. It quite distresses us to hear of the difficulty you experience in buying chinaware when we can buy such lovely things so cheaply here. John's description of your rat trap had us in roars of laughter. Have you caught any yet? We have hundreds of rats around outside, hence our two cats.

John has kept us well supplied with letters during his holiday so now it is our turn to give him equal entertainment during term time. Last week we spent unpacking some of the stores given by the China Relief and the Red Cross Society and getting the x-ray apparatus and generator working. The tube of the larger of the two x-ray plants had become displaced in travelling and we had to take the head to pieces. It was full of transformer oil and we were afraid the casket would leak but, so far, none has come out. The generator gave some trouble but now seems to be working satisfactorily. I am hoping we shall be able to connect up the operating theatre and delivery room for lighting.

Chaotung Hospital entrance.

Chaotung Hospital Outpatients' entrance.

Dr Wang still hasn't arrived and until he comes I shall have no definite programme of work in the hospital. Dr Galbraith plans to go on a trip to the River Miao on November 8th and she is getting ready to hand over the accounts to Winnie.

Last Sunday we held our postponed Harvest Festival. The church was decorated just like an English one. The red peppers and golden maize (corn-on-the-cob) make a beautiful sight. Winnie played the organ and got a fright when she discovered one of the hymns had two more lines per verse than the music, however, she managed very well.

Fields outside Chaotung.

John asks for some details about our daily life. Here are a few to begin with. We try to get up as soon as it is light, about six to six thirty, and do some language study for about half an hour. Our hot water comes at about six forty five and we wash and dress, then have a quiet time until breakfast at seven thirty. After breakfast we have a one-hour language lesson each. At ten o'clock we have tea and cake or biscuits and then carry on with language study on our own until noon. In the afternoon we work in the hospital. Between three and four in the afternoon, we have a light tea with cake and then return to our work. At six it is dark and we have dinner then and go to the sitting room and read, write, knit or sew until about nine thirty, when we go to bed.

HOSPITAL COMPOUND

CHAOTUNG 1948

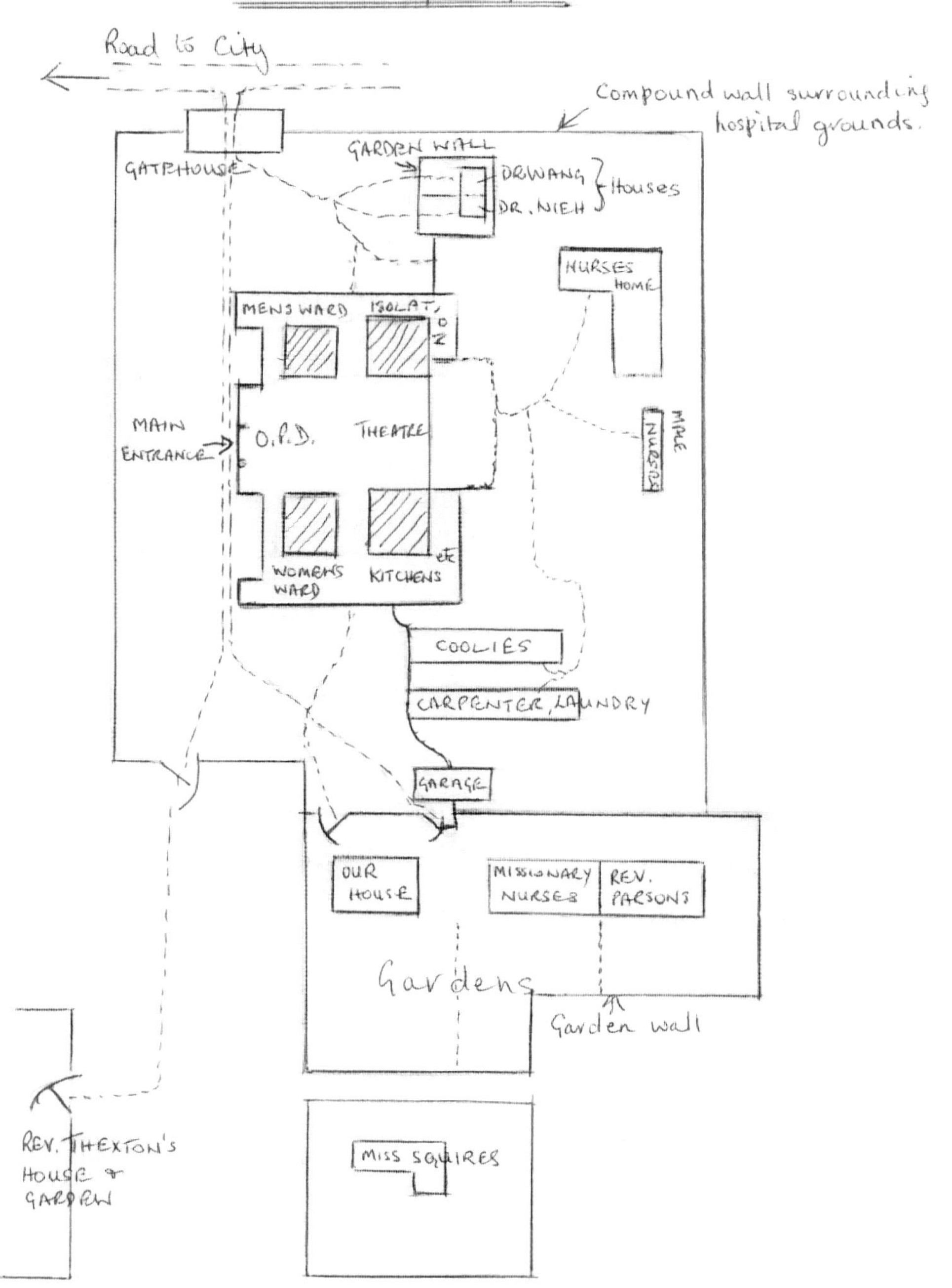

GROUND FLOOR OF HOSPITAL

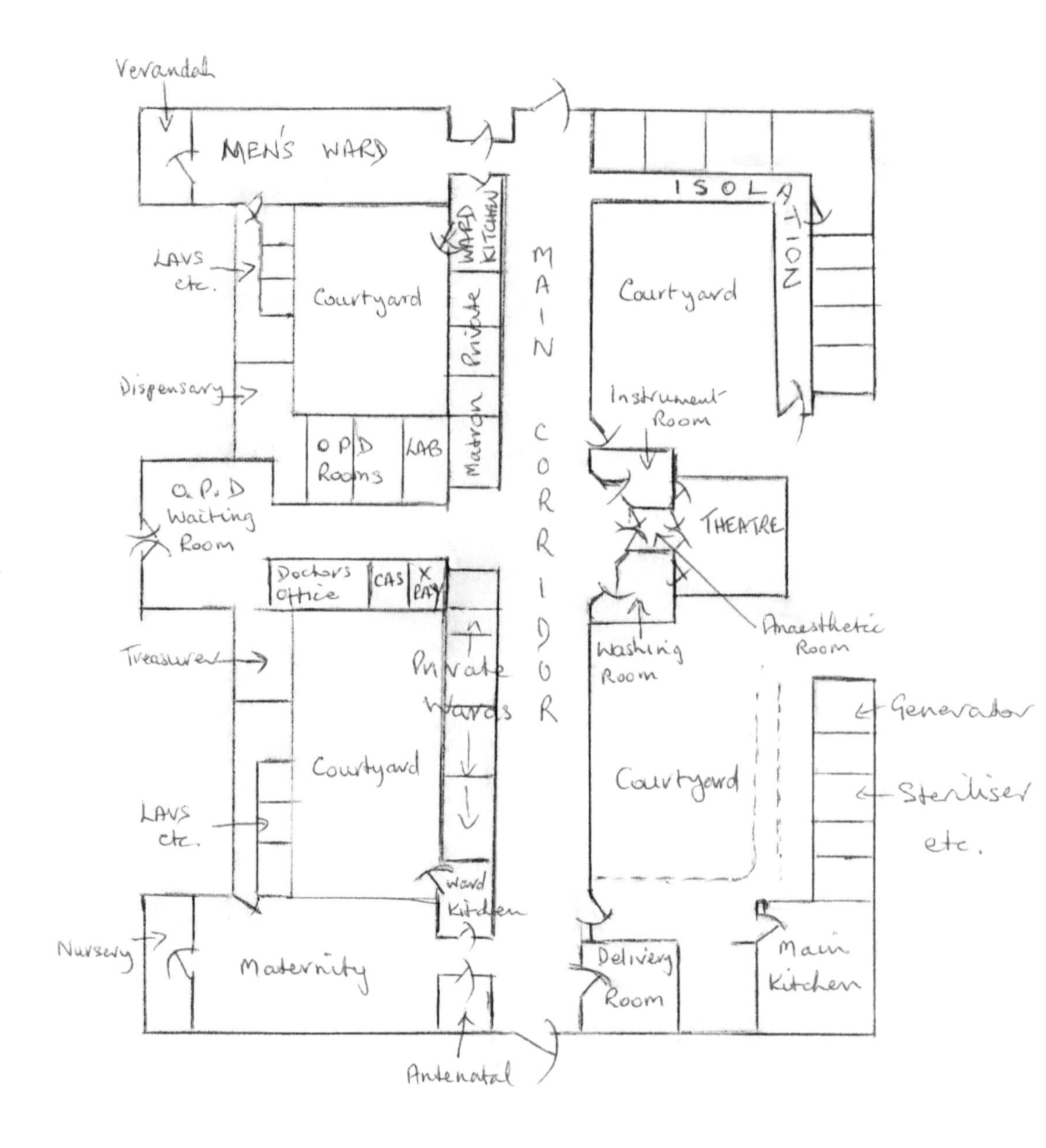

October 26th 1948 - letter from Chaotung to Frank's brother, John.

Winnie:-

Since our arrival in Chaotung, Frank and I have gone right through the hospital stores, lots and lots of wonderful gifts and instruments from the International Red Cross and American Red Cross. We have taken an X-ray head to pieces and straightened the tube, replaced all the oil and it does not leak and, more to the point,-it works well. At the moment Frank is busy wiring the generator to the X-ray room, we do not know what the next job will be.

How you would enjoy the countryside! Yesterday we went to a place about two and a half hours walk across the plain to the foothills, called Da Lung Tung. There we found a river, trees, and a temple with a cave and grotto. In a village nearby we ate a lovely Chinese meal. I had a Hwa Gan (a unique type of carrying chair) and Frank shared two horses with Mr and Mrs Thexton. He enjoyed galloping off and turning back to rejoin us. I walked half the way there and back. I even sat on one of the horses for about five minutes with Frank leading him for me. Later we will return to take some photographs and give you a much better idea of the setting.

You asked how I did the washing. I must confess that I do none apart from stockings and socks. I do the mending myself, make curtains and clothes, but I don't do housework, apart from odds and ends. I study Chinese all morning and in the afternoons I type the hospital notices and letters. Tomorrow, I shall be taking over the Hospital accounts. Each day I take accounts with the cook, which is an awful business as now the new currency which started in August is going just as crazy as the old currency. Shao Ban (silver dollars) three days ago was seven million yuan, today it is ten million.

What else can I think of to justify no housework? Filing for Frank, some gardening in spare time, take nurses choir practice, play for Sunday services at the Chinese Church, keep an eye on the servants and make sure that various jobs are done. In a week or two I shall start issuing the Hospital drugs every day and that's about all.

You also ask, 'What do we eat?' For breakfast today we had porridge, eggs and fried bread, toast and marmalade, or pumpkin jam, with coffee. Dinner was shepherd's pie and cabbage, stewed pears and rice pudding, tea. I forgot elevenses at ten o'clock. Tea is at three and at six o'clock we shall have supper, which I expect will be something like soup, joint of pork with runner beans, cabbage and potatoes, jam pudding and custard, followed by tea. Every day we eat food as good as you will be having at home, and it is not rationed. Sometimes we have a Chinese meal but the cook tends to give us such a good one that it is more expensive than our 'foreign' meals. When we get our garden organised we shall be able to provide most of our own vegetables, apart from potatoes. The cook makes bread using potato yeast. When we send our list of things wanted I shall include a list of seeds. The other day I planted some cabbage seedlings and about half an hour later it rained, they look fine now.

(The soil in Chaotung was very fertile and almost anything would grow. The garden was amply stocked with pear, apple, plum and peach trees as well as strawberry plants.)

The source of our domestic water in Chaotung.

The people in this part of China are much more backward than in Central China. They have yet to be educated in many branches of hospital work. Yesterday, a man was admitted with a fractured os calcis. We X-rayed him in the evening and came home and decided on the best course of treatment. We told him this morning and he has gone home because we cannot promise that immediately after the operation he will be cured. He is a Government Official of some kind, quite wealthy and an opium addict. If the patient refuses the suggested kind of treatment you can do no more and just have to let them go. Sometimes it is very frustrating.

<u>October 26th 1948</u> - letter from Chaotung to Frank's parents.

Winnie:-

Frank began a letter to you the other day and, so far, has got no further with it than a scrap of paper on which he has written the following notes - 'garden, language, instruments, nurses, Thursday operation'. These I will attempt to enlarge upon to the best of my ability.

Garden: As you know we have a large one and last Saturday we both spent a lovely afternoon out in the sunshine collecting cabbage and lettuce seeds and generally trying to tidy things up. Later we hope to be able to grow most of our own vegetables.

Language: Last Monday we both started language study and spent the whole morning studying. Our teacher is a dear old Chinese Minister, and he is very clear with his tones and pronunciation. Some words are different from those in Hankow, for instance where we would say 'ssu' in Hankow dialect, in Chaotung we should say 'shu', and for tea, where in Hankow one would say 't'a' in Chaotung it is 'ch'a'. However, these differences do not mean that we are not understood here, in fact, our cook understands everything we say to him.

Theatre instruments: Last week we both spent two afternoons in the operating theatre going through all the instruments and arranging them properly on the shelves, we also brought new ones down from the storeroom and made up various deficiencies. I have typed a list stating which instruments should be kept on each of the shelves and the nurses should now be able to keep them in order.

Nurses: Two days ago our only two staff nurses walked out. They have apparently been giving quite a lot of trouble because they wanted to be sent elsewhere for further training. They have been told that unless they give one year's service after qualifying they should not expect to be sent anywhere. After talking and reasoning with them they still decided they did not want to stay here, so we had no option but to let them go. We are now left without trained nurses apart from Miss Ma, who is Sister Tutor-cum-Matron-cum-Midwife-cum-Theatre Sister. She is really a grand person and one of the few Chinese who has become a missionary to her own people. We are writing to Kunming to see if anyone there can help us obtain another two trained nurses. Mostly the girls find life very dull and slow in Chaotung and, once trained, they like to get away to the more up-to-date and civilised parts of the country.

Thursday operation: The real details are beyond me, but I do know Frank did an operation on a patient who had osteomyelitis of the sternum. The diseased bone was fairly extensive. I think the man had quite a long history. In the morning Frank did a hernia and all went off well. The theatre itself is quite well run and everybody is very willing to help.

Three cheers! Some papers have just arrived and inside two of them were a pair of socks and some elastic. Very many thanks. Yesterday, I wrote a letter to John and it gives more details about our everyday life, although I did forget to tell you how the Chinese do their washing. If washing for themselves they usually find the nearest stream or pond, no matter how dirty the water, squat down and squeeze the clothes full of water very vigorously on to any rock or stone; otherwise, they use a wooden tub and cold water and just agitate the clothes up and down for ages.

When washing our clothes they use hot water and soap in the same way, rinsing afterwards in clean warm water. We hang our clothes on a line as in England but the Chinese hang theirs on bushes, lay them on rocks or stick a bamboo pole through the sleeves or legs of a garment and prop it up somewhere.

Food: All Chinese food is chopped into small pieces and fried, needing only one pan for frying and one for boiling the rice, it saves a lot of washing up! Our cooks are very good at managing foreign food with all its odds and ends and we have very good meals indeed.

This afternoon I have written a whole pile of letters whilst Frank has been in the rafters of the Hospital trying to wire up the generator to the X-ray plant. We have used the plant twice with great success and our taking it to pieces does not seem to have done any harm. In a few minutes the boy will have the hot water ready for our baths and then it will be suppertime at eight o'clock.
With love to you all, Winnie.

Sunday October 30th 1948 - letter from Chaotung.

Frank:-

Today, apart from morning language study, I've been electrician, laying a cable from the X-ray generator to the X-ray room and wiring the room. I've also connected up the old electricity system of the hospital to the generator and am gradually checking up on the wiring. The hospital used to get electricity from the town but this supply is no longer available. It is going to be a great help to have the hospital wired again but I'm afraid petrol is so short, and so expensive at fifteen shillings a gallon, that we shall only be able to use it in emergencies. Yesterday we had a disappointment when the generator once again refused to start. I think this time it is dirt in the petrol, so we are filtering it before trying to start up once more.

It is surprising how much of one's time is filled with non-medical things; mending appliances, unpacking boxes, doing odd carpentry, mending the truck and so on. The hospital is not busy now, apart from maternity only a third full because of harvest time, so it is a good opportunity to do these odd jobs.

It is a lovely sunny afternoon. I am sitting in our upstairs sitting room by the fire. Winnie is playing some gramophone records. From the window I can see the mountains, today they look black and brown in the sun.

View across the Chaotung plain.

It is often very difficult to persuade patients to have the treatment that one suggests. On Monday a wealthy man, Head of one of the Provincial Government Departments, was attacked by robbers and sustained a fracture of his os calcis. He, like the majority of people here, was an opium addict. Because I told him that he would have to spend two months in bed and that I couldn't make him better in one day by operating, he ordered a chair and went home without treatment. Next day a man came with a bullet in his chest. Because I couldn't take the bullet out, he left and went home, although he needed an operation for removal of an infected rib. The Chinese are used to prescribing their own treatment and like to go from doctor to doctor until they get what they want. We refuse to give injections unless really needed.

Despite the change of currency on August 19th inflation has continued and during the last two weeks things have trebled in price. The pernicious thing is the Chinese Government still keeps the exchange at about twelve dollars to the pound sterling, when the real value is forty dollars a pound. They must be making a lot of money out of this situation. The Mission gave us a grant of one thousand pounds sterling to repair the earthquake damage. By the time the Bank had remitted it in Chinese dollars from Kunming (ten days ago) to Chaotung, it was worth eight hundred pounds only. We are expecting the Chinese part of our salary to be doubled to meet the emergency.

You will have realised from the above that the rate of inflation had been very troublesome for some time. Even when we were living in Hankow in August 1948 the Chinese Government had tried to stabilise the currency at twelve Yuan to the pound sterling, and by October 1948 things were really going haywire. The exchange rate was increasing at a tremendous speed. Keeping track of our personal affairs was difficult enough, but when it came to hospital accounts, matters were even more complicated. By March 1949 the rate had risen to thirty-six million yuan to one pound sterling. Payment for missionary personnel stipends was sent from England to the bank in Kunming then transferred directly to the bank in Chaotung. Grants for hospital work were forwarded in a similar way.

Under normal circumstances this system worked very well as the local Bank Manager would immediately notify the hospital that the money had arrived and pay it over. However, once the dramatic exchange rates began to take place overnight, a loophole appeared. The Chaotung bank would receive money one day, keep it overnight, then notify us of its arrival the following day. In the meantime, the exchange rate could have risen alarmingly. The canny bank manager would hand over the amount to us calculated at the rate at which he had received it the previous evening, thus keeping the extra 'inflation gain' for himself.

Our patients all paid a small fee to the hospital for their treatment and also bought the prescribed drugs from the hospital. The only way that we could keep abreast with the fast moving exchange rate was to gather up all the cash taken each evening, then go out on the street and buy sacks of rice, brown sugar lumps or bales of cloth, indeed anything that could be stored and sold later at the going rate. In addition, old Chinese silver dollars were purchased, whenever there were sufficient funds, because their value remained stable.

The sugar, rice and cloth were stored in the loft of our house until such time as we required more cash, then they could be sold at the current rate of exchange. In this way we endeavoured to avoid losing large amounts of valuable money. For me it meant hours of extra work keeping the account books in good order.

One very amusing unforeseen snag occurred as a result of these arrangements. On climbing out of bed one morning I attempted to put my feet into my slippers and my toes came into contact with something hard and knobbly. Whatever could it be? Imagine my surprise when I found three or four lumps of brown sugar nestling inside the toecap. We puzzled about this for a while, then I found a few more lumps inside one of the badly fitting drawers in the chest-of-drawers. How could they possibly have got there? We had heard no noises during the night. Over the next day or so we kept coming across small piles of sugar around the house and finally arrived at the conclusion that the rats, who lived in the attic, must be responsible. It took us quite a time to work out how they could get from the roof and into the bedroom. Eventually we discovered that they simply ran down the ladder that gave us access to the attic, which was easy, because there was no trapdoor.

I was not very keen on the idea of rats running around in the house during the night. We tried to control their numbers, but the hospital compound was surrounded on three sides by miles of maize fields and it was virtually impossible to keep them out of the house.

We tried many ways to protect the hospital from inflation, and towards the end of our stay we attempted to avoid the problem of transferring money to the bank. In order to do this before the roads were completely cut off, a consignment of silver dollars was packed into a wooden box and hidden in a secret compartment under the mission lorry on its last journey from Kunming. The lorry was held up in transit for a week or more by bandits. When the lorry eventually arrived in Chaotung it was important to keep its contents secret because of the risk of burglary but, unfortunately, when unloading the box, which was extremely heavy, our deaf gardener dropped it on the ground, the dollars spilt out so everybody knew and the secret was out.

<u>November 14th 1948</u> - letter from Chaotung.

Frank:-

At last Dr. Wang has arrived from Wanshien. Winnie and I were walking back from a wedding feast yesterday about half past five when we saw him, with his wife and child, standing at the Gatehouse. We are indeed glad that he has arrived. They have a very pleasant little house and already seem to be settling in well.

The wedding yesterday was like most Chinese ones held in church. The ceremony was officially charted as starting at twelve noon so we planned to go about three thirty in the afternoon, which in China would be about right. But at two o'clock a messenger came out to 'Ch'ing' us to come as the bride and bridegroom had arrived. The wedding eventually began at three o'clock. On the platform stood the Minister and on one side sat the bridegroom's father and his middleman. The bride, bridegroom, bridesmaids and best man stood in front, as we do. In one corner stood the Announcer, or Master of Ceremonies. First of all he announced the crackers and off they went, then he announced the organ and Winnie played a twiddly bit; finally, he announced the wedding service and the Minister began.

The bride's father, a real old style gentleman, arrived late in accordance with his dignity and the service was stopped while he found his place on the platform. Winnie had to play two hymns, which nobody knew. Nobody had hymnbooks either so they were more or less organ voluntaries. After the service the bride and bridegroom bowed a lot to different people and then went out to have their photographs taken. After all this there followed a good, but simple, feast.

(This is a good opportunity to mention that quite often the bride and groom could not read or write, so the officiating minister would carry the service, 'filling in' himself where necessary whether it be the organ playing, crackers banging, or the bride and groom's vows.)

Inflation steadily gets worse and there are rumours that sterling will soon get an exchange rate of forty-eight Chinese dollars to the pound sterling, instead of twelve. Cost of living has gone up five times since August, and rice went up fifty per cent overnight last week. If we get the new exchange rate, and the one hundred percent Mission House bonus, we ourselves shall not suffer. We are still much better off in many ways, such as food and fuel and servants than you are in England, but the hospital and Chinese people are badly affected by all this.

Chaotung is a city built on a slight hill in the middle of a plain surrounded by mountains. Around it, like all the towns in Yunnan, is a high wall, and North, South, East and West are gates with big watchtowers above. The gates are closed at night.

Chaotung main street with East Gate behind.

A lot of the population live in houses outside the wall. The roads are very rough and muddy, and are made especially dirty by all the packhorses carrying coal through from the mines. We have just heard that sterling is going to exchange at sixty dollars to the pound. More than we expected, so things will be easier now.

Dr Galbraith is going on a trip to the River Miao people tomorrow and will be away four weeks. The guide who came to meet her was a week late. He fell in with Government soldiers who compelled him to turn back and carry their luggage and then robbed him. They even took the letter he was carrying to Dr Galbraith with instructions for the journey.

<u>December 5th 1948</u> - letter from Chaotung.

Frank:-

Please forgive the fortnight's lapse in letter writing. We have been particularly busy and no spare moment in which to write. A few days ago there was a heavy fall of snow and the mountains looked really beautiful. The truck from Kunming was delayed a day and didn't arrive until long after dark on Saturday. The snow, and the mud following its thaw, made the journey very difficult. They finally got completely stuck about half a mile from the hospital and came on by foot. Coolies unloaded the truck in the morning and brought the luggage onto the compound, then the truck managed to get out of the mud by its own power. There were four new arrivals to the District on the truck - Win Sanderson from Hupeh who has come to help us with the nursing, Bert and Marjorie Wood, from Bristol, (although I have not met them before) and Chris Smith, once Senior Prefect at Kingswood School and a friend of John's. They were together in the Friends' Ambulance Unit at Failand (situated somewhere near Bristol).

This week I visited our Leper Home and Dispensary at Stone Gateway about twenty-five miles away. I went with Ken Parsons who was going to inspect the work on the new missionaries' houses there. We left shortly after eight o'clock in the morning on Wednesday.

Ken had a stallion called 'Prince', and another packhorse. He used to travel to remote places for weeks at a time, giving magic lantern shows about Bible stories as well as sometimes giving inoculations and simple eye treatment. On the occasions that Frank rode Prince, it would be an adventurous ride. Prince could sense the novice on his back and took advantage, going off in his own chosen direction if he scented a nearby mare.

After about three quarters of an hour's ride over the plain we got off our horses to climb the first small coal hill. This is a smallish mountain with outcrops of coal all over it. We climbed into freezing mist and all the bushes and grass looked very pretty, encased in transparent cylinders of ice.

After the small coal hill came the big coal hill and then we went up another hill with several swallet holes on it, one being called the 'bottomless pit'. From there we crossed a plain covered with pines and entered a gorge. We climbed up one side over a landslide caused by the earthquake, and then found ourselves high up, looking down into the Stone Gateway valley. High mountains surround the valley. The Mission Compound with Schools, Rural Development Centre, Church and Dispensary is high up on one side. At one end of the valley is the Leper Home and high up at the other end is the Orphanage. The Mission owns all the land around and some of the mountain too.

Stone Gateway was established in 1905 by Samuel Pollard, a missionary from the Bible Christian Churches of the West Country (Cornwall and Devon). The history can be found in Elliot Kendall's book 'Beyond the Clouds'. Ken and his twin brother Keith were born at Stone Gateway when their parents worked there a few years after Pollard's death.

The Leper Home is really a sad sight. Many of the buildings are down due to the earthquake, and the lepers are living in crude shelters. I saw all the lepers on Thursday morning. They are badly in need of better medical care and very little is being done in the way of curative treatment. In the afternoon I visited a sick woman, inspected the new houses and helped test some of the chimneys and then had an interview with the Dispenser. We returned in glorious warm sunshine on Friday morning and arrived home at a gallop at about two o'clock. We then had x-rays to do, a birthday party to go to and an official welcome meeting at the hospital to attend.

We are getting more patients now. My first cataract patient here is going out tomorrow and can see well. The second is going to need a needling - he is an opium addict and not very cooperative. It is fun trying to do sight testing - so far I've had two patients. (I guess the fun part was difficulty with language!) *Maternity keeps me quite busy - I was busy all yesterday with blood transfusions for a severe haemorrhage.*

<u>December 12th 1948</u> - letter from Chaotung.

Winnie:-

We usually attend the church service held in the Middle School right near the hospital. This church is badly neglected, it has no windows, the majority of them having been stolen, all the doors are in such bad condition that they will not shut at all and we have to wear all our warmest clothes. For lighting we have a pressure lamp slung from a rope, and the hymns are written in large characters on a sheet, which is hung up on the platform. Between fifty and sixty schoolboys attend the service, also some of the nurses.

Frank has just come in and said, 'What can we give the little baby whose mother cannot feed him?' They are buying cow's milk, from the vendor at the gatehouse, which looks just like water with a little whitener in it. I have given him one of my five-pound tins of powdered milk and hope that, by the time that is used up, the mother will be able to afford a wet nurse.

These sorts of problems crop up every few days. In the Maternity Ward the other day a wee baby died from Haemorrhagic Disease of the Newborn. This very morning, all the patients but one went home, they were afraid that the spirit of the dead baby would haunt them. These poor, ignorant people, their lives are so much ruled by fear and superstition.

To turn to a more cheerful subject, we are busy getting ready for Christmas, the nurses are practising carols and a Christmas play, and we are to plan the games for their party on the 29th December. In addition, there will be a dinner for missionaries at the Thexton's house and afterwards they are all coming to our house for games, ours being the largest house on the compound. And to think that only last year, we spent Christmas on board ship!

<u>December 12th 1948</u> - letter from Chaotung.

> *Frank:-*
>
> *It is now a fortnight to Christmas and, though it may be too late, we should like to wish you all a very, very happy Christmas and New Year. Mother's letter of 25th November came today. It was written in Bath and tells us of the death of Auntie Lucy - this is a great surprise to us both.*
>
> *This week the hospital has kept both of us busy and we have had much less time for language study. We've spent quite a lot of time in the x-ray room - the time switch on the machine has been wrong and often the films have not been exposed and have had to be taken many times over. We had one maternity patient who needed a blood transfusion and I have had quite a lot of small operating to do. I am getting more practice with the use of the cystoscope and sigmoidoscope.*
>
> *This week our cook has gone off to buy a new cow and his brother is cooking instead. He is deaf and dumb and we have great fun making ourselves understood. This morning he served cheese on toast, instead of butter. But he is really doing very well.*

Entrance to Little Dragon Cave.

Yesterday, we took the day off to celebrate our wedding anniversary. Win Sanderson, Winnie and I went to a place called 'Little Dragon Cave'. We got up early in the morning and left soon after breakfast. The two Wins had 'Hwa Gans', carrying chairs made of two long bamboo poles with two cross struts and a hammock made of bamboo slats; quite simple but very comfortable.

I remember that Frank had padded my 'Hwa Gan' so well with a sleeping bag that my hips would not sink between the two poles and I was lying flat along the top.

I rode Ken Parson's horse, Prince, a fine sandy coloured stallion, and thoroughly enjoyed myself. Hsiao Lung Tung was twenty li (about eight miles) away.

We first crossed the plains, sometimes following the bullock cart track and sometimes on banks between rice fields. We then climbed the foothills and walked a little way up the mountain to the house, which is kept as a holiday house for missionaries. It is being repaired and put in order, but a few more earthquake shocks this last week have done quite a lot of damage. We sat in the garden and ate a picnic lunch.

After this we walked over to the Small Dragon Cave - a cave with a stream running through. It was once a temple but now the buildings are being used to make fireproof, unglazed cooking vessels. There was a huge furnace built into the earth and, behind the fire, sat a woman working some huge bellows. The fumes from the burning coals were dreadful but the people working there seemed quite unconcerned.

Entrance to
Big Dragon Cave.

We returned to the house and after a snack of oranges we set off again for home. It was a lovely day, eleven hours of sunshine without a cloud in the sky. A few of the distant mountains were already snow capped. We now have this gloriously clear, sunny weather every day, and it should last until after Christmas.

Our money arrived this week and we are now quite rich. For a long time we were short and this remittance is making up for the back deficiencies, as well as covering our future needs. Postage has suddenly jumped once again and has become a heavy item.

December 19th 1948 - letter from Chaotung.

Frank:-

Synod is immediately after Christmas and Winnie has just been balancing the hospital books in readiness. We have been quite busy this week and nowadays are getting more operating to do. Next Tuesday for instance, we shall have an arthroplasty of elbow, excision of carcinoma of face, pterygium and iridectomy, needling for after cataract and a biopsy of tumour to do. The gynaecology clinic is growing - I had six sterility cases for investigation last Thursday. The X-ray apparatus is working better too and last time we made some quite good films.

At this time I was acting as X-ray assistant and worked in the dark room as well. I also gave general anaesthetics when needed. We were constantly meeting unexpected circumstances and sometimes learnt the hard way. Heating in the hospital was minimal and in the operating theatre an open, charcoal-burning fire was used. During the operating sessions we wondered why, every now and again, a nurse would 'pass-out'. Suddenly, it dawned on us that charcoal fumes and ether make rather a potent mixture. We did overcome this problem but I cannot remember how.

Yesterday we went into the city for a little Christmas shopping and had an enjoyable time haggling over prices. The hospital is making great preparations for Christmas. Winnie is responsible for the nurses' party and for the missionaries' party, which is going to be held in our house as we have two rooms, which can be thrown into one. Next week, in between times, I am going to try and get the wiring for one of the wards done so that we can have a film show on Christmas Day.

We are all thinking of the best plan for the future of the leprosy work. The leper home here was badly damaged by the earthquake and we now have an opportunity for re-planning the work and deciding what sort of building we shall have. At present, Stone Gateway is so far away from Chaotung that the lepers get little medical care and we are hoping that it may be possible to rebuild the home with a small hospital and that we shall be able to appoint one of our nurses to supervise the work there.

You would be very amused to see us climbing up into our bed at night. Winnie has made a straw mattress and it is so thick that it sits on top of the bed like icing on a cake. It will soon settle down though. Winnie has just finished making a winter dress too, which looks very smart, and is now making some blouses.

The nurses make all the decorations in the wards. They buy white paper and dye it. One ward has chrysanthemums, which look absolutely real.

One of my jobs in the near future will be to mend the hospital harmonium. It leaks so badly that one can hardly keep up with pumping. I hope to stick some leather on with glue and make it right again.
Now, goodbye for another week.
Love, Frank.

These snippets give an insight into how all missionaries were called upon to tackle any emergency. We were very isolated, therefore we had to be self-reliant, for instance making our own straw mattress in order to avoid getting bed bug infestation.

In the following letter you will see how, when the nurses walked out on strike leaving nobody to work on the wards, all the missionary personnel came to the rescue with the general nursing care.

<u>December 26th 1948</u> - letter from Chaotung.

Frank:-

The week began with a Nurses' strike on Tuesday. All the girl nurses walked out and mobbed the boy nurses so that they could not work either. They went for a day's outing to the Big Dragon Cave. We gathered all the missionaries together and in the morning they all did the ward work. In the afternoon we did nine operations and went on until seven-thirty. Then at nine o'clock, we held a staff meeting and afterwards met the nurses. Everyone went to bed eventually long after midnight. On Wednesday the nurses were persuaded to come on duty and in the afternoon another staff meeting was held, then at seven-thirty the nurses were seen again

They presented a demand of thirteen trivial and very petty points. These were discussed until midnight and then the matter was finally closed. Dr. Nieh and Miss Ma were so ill after this that they could not come on duty. Dr. Nieh returned yesterday afternoon but Miss Ma is still in bed, so in this way all our own Christmases were very haphazard. However, despite this, the nurses gave a nativity play in the morning at eleven o'clock. They came to us at ten o'clock saying they had no costumes so we rushed around, collected clothes from everybody and managed to dress them up; we even got haloes for the 'angels' - in appearance only! After the play, Father Christmas (Leslie Thexton) gave out presents in the wards, then we had lunch and went to service in the city.

I have had two interesting operations this week, and Winnie assisted me at both. The first was a cancer of the cheek and the second, arthroplasty of elbow. Both cases are doing well though the former insists on going home even before his stitches are out.

December 26th letter continued.

Winnie:-

Christmas preparations were greatly disrupted by the nurses' strike. The nurses are youngsters between sixteen and eighteen years of age and have no sense of responsibility to one another. There were one or two chief 'spokesmen' amongst them whom I believe caused the trouble. It is unfortunate that it happened during Christmas week as it has meant a terrific scramble for us, especially with Dr.Nieh and Miss Ma both off-duty afterwards. I am becoming professional assistant surgeon!

Today we've been completely free from work and managed a walk after church service. This afternoon there were seven adult baptisms. Christmas Day service started three-quarters of an hour late, of necessity I had to play quite a recital on the organ. Luckily I had taken a fair amount of music with me and was able to keep going throughout.

You would have laughed to see the cook bring up a live chicken to the sitting room telling us it was his present to us, Frank was so surprised - he put out his hand to stroke it's head!

Letter: 19th January 19th 1949 - letter from Chaotung.

Winnie:-

Well, Synod is now over and all the visitors started on their three-day truck journey back to Kunming yesterday morning. It was a bitterly cold day and the truck was absolutely loaded to capacity. Altogether there were about fifty people crowded on top of the luggage, we did not envy them their journey across the mountains, most of them wore so many clothes that all one could see were noses.

Synod has been an enjoyable, though very busy, time. Wives cannot attend the meetings unless in an official capacity. The only session Frank and I had to attend was the Medical one; Frank, because he is the missionary doctor, and I, because I am the Hospital Treasurer. Apart from this Dr. Nieh has represented the hospital, for which he had time off, this left Frank too busy.

Three or four meetings were held in our house. We opened up the partition between our dining and sitting rooms downstairs and on the first Sunday the English service and communion were held there. It was good to hear a sermon in English. As yet we get no help from Chinese sermons, our understanding of the language still being limited. On Tuesday, also in our house, the 'Missionaries Meeting' and tea was held (about thirty of us). The meeting commenced at two o'clock in the afternoon and, with a break for supper, went on until ten thirty. On Thursday we met together again for tea, which included an auction sale of goods left behind by a missionary who is not returning to the field. In addition to these meetings all sorts of people were popping in and out of our house, it being the nearest, for odd cups of tea. Every lunch time we entertained two Chinese guests, and consequently enjoyed some good Chinese meals.

Yesterday Dr. Nieh commenced a month's holiday, which leaves Frank and Dr. Wang to carry on all the work by themselves. Dr. Galbraith went off on the Synod truck for her furlough. I am doing less and less in the hospital as I find I get tired very quickly this means that I am able to catch up on knitting and sewing in readiness for baby's due date, April 29th.

It is good to receive your letters every week. We are finding it difficult to send airmail to England as the postage has now risen to forty dollars and the post office does not have sufficient large denomination stamps to put on them.

There is quite a lot of unrest going on round about owing to the changing situation of the Government. We are just staying put and hoping for the best. The truck is being brought back from Kunming and is to be kept at this end of the District in case we have to evacuate at any time. We are so far away from civilisation that possibly we do not realise how serious things are, however, perhaps this is all to the good as we just do not worry about it.

Note added by Frank:-

> *The Synod time has been very interesting. For the first time we met many of the Chinese, Nosu and Miao ministers from the country churches.*

January 21st 1949 - letter continued.

Winnie:-

The situation in the City is very hectic, people are nervous of what will happen to the Government, and prices are going up and up. Two days ago the cook bought a box of soap for two hundred and seventy Chinese dollars. Yesterday he bought another for three hundred and fifty, while one shop asked six hundred. Three days ago coal was twenty dollars a basket, today, it's eighty. What chance is there of keeping hospital fees up-to-date and thus making the hospital pay its way? We change the fees and drug prices often enough as it is.

January 23rd 1949 - letter from Chaotung.

> *Frank:-*
>
> *Please forgive me if I begin this letter with requests - if I finish with them first I can go on to news. Firstly, my shoes are wearing out more quickly than I thought. If Pugsleys can remember my fitting would they please supply two pairs, one black and one brown. Should Pugsleys not remember, I will get the Roman Catholic training school in Kunming to make some.*

(This is indicative as to the amount of walking we did, going from one place to another, mostly along very rough and rugged paths.)

> *Next, please thank Aunty May and Aunty Irene very much for their kind Christmas presents. We were very touched John, with your letter about 'OXO' and his kind donation. Winnie and I have been thinking about the*

best use for it and we think it would be well used to buy some medical books in England for Dr. Wang. He has turned out to be a grand colleague. He works day and night and is very, very keen about his work. Medical books are extremely difficult to obtain out here and some from England would be a great help to him and so, indirectly, to the hospital too. Incidentally, if you are sending any more goods as 'medical supplies' we are trying to arrange for them to be brought out as Relief Supplies duty free. At the moment there is a complete veto on many goods and terrific customs charges on others.

We have been very thrilled with the accounts of Kin Sen's performance as Henrietta - it has even appeared in the Newspapers arriving from Home.

Kin Sen, one of Aunty May's Chihuahua dogs, appeared in 'The Scarlet Pimpernel' and Aunty donated some of the income from this to the hospital in Chaotung.

It is wonderful of Aunty May to make us so generous a gift. We have been struggling so hard to make ends meet in the hospital - it will be invaluable to know that there is a fund at home, which can be used to draw on to buy supplies from England. Otherwise, it would mean a reduction in our grant from home on which we depend so greatly to make good the deficit in the hospital income from fees.

Mr. Orme at Elstree asks about the type of cases we get in the hospital. Many of the outpatients are septic skin cases, often due to scabies, and we use large quantities of gentian violet and ammoniated mercury ointment. Quite a large number of patients have eye diseases, most due to trachoma and its complications. Dr. Wang is doing the eye work and becoming very proficient. We also see a lot of Venereal Disease. The Miao nearly all have congenital syphilis, a heritage from their pre-

Christian days, and the Chinese, especially the addicts, are frequently infected. Tuberculosis is very frequently seen. In season we have typhoid, typhus, dysentery, malaria, relapsing fever and smallpox. At the moment pneumonia is common.

In the Wards are many burns, especially of children who fall into the open fires, which are placed on the ground in the centre of their dwellings. There is a great deal of opium smoking. In addition, we have the same range of conditions as in England and one has to be a jack-of-all-trades.

Last weekend we were invited to dinner with the local Mandarin (Hsien Chang). He wanted us to help equip the new Municipal Hospital. At the present time it is an impressive looking building, big enough for three hundred beds. The doors and windows are not yet in. They want us to make a list of equipment so that they can know what to buy. To date they have no nurses, only one doctor and a business manager so they are going to have a very difficult time getting it going.

Dr. Nieh has gone on holiday this week. He is hoping to rescue his brother who has been captured by bandits, there's no telling how long he will be away. Dr. Wang and I are managing the hospital. I have a dear old lady, Miss Li, acting as interpreter. She is Chaotung's first nurse, and has been to England. She is sister to our language teacher.

Next week is Kuor Nien (or the Chinese New Year) when everybody takes a holiday. All the patients, whether cured or not, try to go home, all the shops are shut and nobody works. Everyone pays visits, gives presents and attends feasts. Winnie, on her way to church today (I was on duty) saw pigs being killed everywhere in readiness - she saw them being de-haired, skinned and cut up. Our cook has been buying in large quantities of stores in readiness for the shops closing.

We don't know what is going to result from Chiang Kai-Chek's resignation and the Government's surrender. Some are fearful and think we may have to leave China, whilst others; Leslie Thexton and our Chairman included, think work will go on as usual. Winnie and I are just trusting that we shall be permitted to stay. There is probably less to be feared here from Communists than from local bandits.

Winnie is thrilled to hear of the Teddy Bear coming from Aunty May. She is very well and is getting into training now, with relaxation exercises and afternoon rests.

This was the time when Huntley Dick-Reed was advocating the idea that being able to relax your body during childbirth was extremely helpful. His idea was that relaxing into the pain rather that fighting it is less painful. I found a lot of truth in what he said and endeavoured to use his method myself.

March 1st 1949 - letter from Chaotung.
Winnie:-
We quite forgot to say "white rabbits" this morning! I think the first thing we said when the alarm went off was, 'Oh dear, is it six o'clock already? Frank has his Chinese lessons at seven o'clock every morning and dear old Rev Li has no watch, so gets up with the sun. Now, on a bright sunny morning, he arrives at six thirty and on a dull day at seven fifteen.

The Rev Li was 72 years of age and lived in the family home surrounded by his children and grandchildren. Every morning, during our lesson period, we would place a tray beside him on which stood tea and biscuits. For a while neither Frank nor I could solve the mystery of the disappearing biscuits. Always, at the end of a lesson the biscuit plate was empty, yet Rev Li had not eaten one. Just out of curiosity, we took particular notice one day and discovered that, every now and again, he would carefully take a biscuit from the plate and put it within the folds of the ample sleeves of his gown. He was, of course, gathering up the biscuits to take home for his grandchildren. Needless to say, we continued to provide a generous supply of biscuits each morning.

The weather has become warm and sunny and most trees are turning green, blossom is coming out, and the peas, beans and other crops planted in the fields earlier are just beginning to show through the soil. They say we shall not get any more really cold weather and it does seem that Spring is here.

The hospital work increases every day. We've just been going through some of the figures, and operations to date have been one hundred and four in 1949, whereas by the same time last year they numbered only fourteen. Outpatients have been one thousand two hundred this year, last year eight hundred. Financially this month the hospital has been able to save a little so, altogether, we feel we are getting somewhere. Dr Wang proves a wonderful colleague and takes part in the spiritual as well as medical side of hospital life.

We have received a statement of our account at Mission House up to October 1948, and this shows that no monies have been remitted home from the Field. This is due to the fact that Central China District has not sent a statement back to Mission House. We have written to the Rev Moody, South West district, asking him to forward the statement and hope things will soon be straightened out.

*We, personally, have about fifty pounds sterling in Hong Kong as we cannot spend anything in Chaotung apart from housekeeping money, and the balance is being sent to England. Each Quarter we stipulate how much we want in Chaotung then so much for home and so much for Hong Kong. This means that when our *half-term break comes, we can do some re-equipping in Hong Kong. We hope that for a year or two we shall be settled here and the money will run smoothly.*

(The half-term break alluded to refers to an arrangement where, after spending two years working in Chaotung at an altitude of nine thousand feet, a period of rest at a lower level was needed.)

Newspapers have not been coming through at all since December and the latest journals we have received are dated October 1948. I expect one day we shall have a huge batch. Letters come quite regularly and I love reading yours.

A fortnight ago, an F.A.U. (Friends' Ambulance Unit) truck arrived out of the blue with some International Red Cross drugs for the hospital. With the truck came two China Inland Mission missionaries from a Leprosarium in Sa La Chi, near Pichieh. Dr. Fish (Canadian) aged seventy, and Dr Oleson (Australian) aged sixty-nine. They had come for a short holiday and stayed with us. They are two 'grand old boys'. Dr Fish and Frank got on famously, and Mr Oleson came round with me doing all my odd jobs. Dr Fish gave us some useful hints about running leper homes. The F.A.U. driver went to Stone Gateway to see the remains of our Leper Home and has now returned to Chungking to see if the F.A.U. will send folk to help with the rebuilding. We are living in hope!

I have been helping Frank in outpatients. Nearly all the cases are interesting in some way or other and the work is most varied. By going into the hospital I see Frank during the day, otherwise, I hardly see him from morning till night.

Most of the things are ready for the baby when he/she arrives. It hardly seems possible that eight weeks from now he/she should be here. Now I must go and dish out the dispensary stores. Lots of love, Winnie.

March 13th 1949 - letter from Chaotung.

Frank:-

To our joy Dr. Nieh has come back, so Dr. Wang and I will have an easier time now. The hospital has not been so busy for many years. A week ago we had a gastroenterostomy, two cataracts, a dissection of T.B. glands of neck and a mastoidectomy, together with smaller operations in a matter of nine days. Next week two salpingostomies and a synovectomy of knee are planned already but I'm afraid it is proving too much for the number of nurses on the staff. Also the laundry and sterilising facilities are hardly adequate to cope with this amount of operative work.

It is good to have Dr.Nieh back. The assistants had been complaining that their wages were insufficient and we had persistently told them to wait until Dr. Nieh returned. There are a lot of hospital repairs and new buildings to be done too, these have been waiting for Dr. Nieh to fix the contract with the builders.

Dr. Nieh was telling us yesterday about his home. It is on a hill like Steep Holm and on the hills all the way round are local bandits and one never feels safe. His brother, who was kidnapped, has been released and the Government has supplied the local people with ammunition with which to fight the bandits.

Our truck has not returned from Kunming. Its departure has been delayed several times because bandits are in possession of part of the road. Many trucks have been robbed and the passengers deprived of all except their underclothing. The money situation has temporarily stabilised again. We now charge silver for hospital fees.

Spring has really come to Yunnan and on warm days it is as hot as an English summer. Our garden has given us many pleasant surprises. There is a peach tree in profuse blossom and a magnolia tree. There are also some trees with white blossom and one with pink blossom like tiny buttons whose names I do not know. Wallflowers and violets are also in bloom.

To our joy John's gardening book arrived this week together with some medical journals, the first printed matter to arrive since December. We hear that nineteen lorries of postal matter are held up in Kweiyang until the roads are cleared of bandits. To tide over the time until our seeds arrive we are planting potatoes, Chinese cabbage, peas and beans. Winnie is also growing some tomato seeds.

Dr. Wang is going to Stone Gateway again next weekend. He very much enjoys these visits and they are greatly appreciated. People come from distant villages in order to receive treatment. He also visit's the Stone Gateway Leper Home and takes Sunday services.

This week we held a committee meeting about the rebuilding of the Leper Home. We are hoping to include a small hospital block alongside, as well as a communal dining room, kitchen and recreation room for men and women.

P.S. Received three letters on Saturday bearing a stamp to say that they had been recovered by P.O. from bandits.

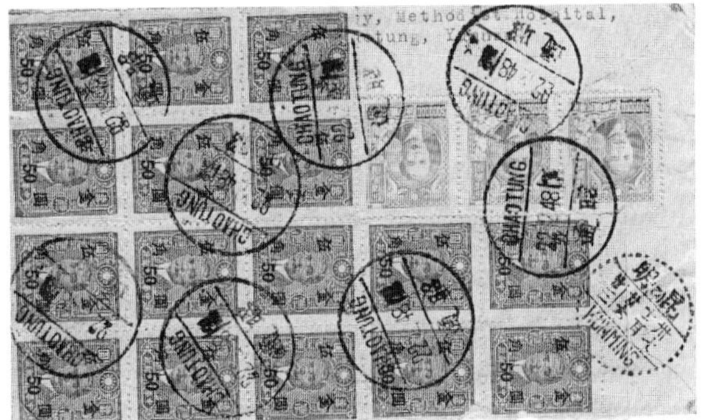

One of the airmail envelopes sent from Chaotung with stamps on both sides.

<u>March 27th 1949</u> – letter from Chaotung to Winnie's mother, Mrs Hill.

Winnie:-

It is a long time now since we sent a letter to you as postage is going up and up and our money cannot come through from Kunming. We hear many stories of bandits on the road and truck traffic is almost at a standstill. We have decided to send this letter and then wait for a week or two before sending any more. Please don't worry about us as we are quite safe here, it is just part of the general unrest prevalent all over China. We heard that, on the 'News' last night, they said peace talks were to begin on April 1st, perhaps if the Nationalists and Communists can reach some agreement things will settle down.

What the final position for missionaries will be we must wait and see. Meanwhile, being so far up country, we carry on as normal, apart from the fact that the folk at Weining are coming to Chaotung. Weining is much more isolated in that there are only Elliott Kendall, his wife and two children, and one teacher on the compound. Today the small truck has gone off to fetch Joan (the teacher), Mrs. Kendall and children. Chris Smith has gone from here to live with Elliott at Weining.

There has been considerable bandit trouble in that area. The story goes that the so called bandits treat the ordinary people well and pay for any food they may take, only ill treating the rich folk. On the other hand, the Government soldiers sweep into an area and just take everything, including cows, pigs, chickens and food, and either eat or sell them without repaying the owners. Consequently, and understandably, the peasants and working class folk have no sympathy with the Government as such. Oh, how often we wish and pray for the sake of the Chinese themselves that some peaceful settlement could be made and the Nation settle down to a few years of happy, steady living.

<u>April 28th 1949</u> - letter from Chaotung to Dorothy Reece, a friend working in Africa.

> *Frank:-*
>
> *At the moment we are in a strange position. Our compound is outside the city wall and for the last two days bandits have been besieging the city for most of the night, on and off during the day we can hear rifle fire. Today, though Easter Sunday, we've had to stay at home or in the hospital. The situation in Yunnan has been very unsettled for some time. For about three months bandits have been stopping trucks on the only good motor road to Kunming. About three weeks ago they surrounded Weining, the nearest large town on the motor road, and from there they went to Huitse and captured the city. This present group of bandits around Chaotung are an independent band coming from the North. We were expecting a 'plane from Kunming on Friday to bring money and drugs, but the arrival of bandits here prevented its coming. Some of the bandits have Communist students amongst them but others are not Communist. We do not know what the Communist attitude to Mission work will be when the peace talks are finished.*
>
> *Our work, however, has been going on much as before until these last few days when the city gates have been closed and patients cannot get out to come to hospital.*

One week later

The bandits besieged the city until Tuesday night and then disappeared as quickly as they had come. They were overtaken and surrounded the day after and many were killed. Whilst there were a few Communists amongst them, most were ordinary peasant folk who had been compelled to come and fight by their feudal lord, a man named Lung. This man, Lung, had recently been punished by the local official for growing opium and in revenge he was trying to capture the official and, if possible, take his place.

We heard today that Nanking has fallen. It is thought here that if the Communists do conquer China, Yunnan will probably become an Independent Province.

The Chinese are a race of individualists and know little of responsibility outside their exacting family claims. They have very little self-discipline, you can never rely on a patient doing as he is told or coming back when he should. They make promises to 'save face' and never keep them. It is a land of compromises. Even our Medical Superintendent, Dr Nieh often compromises by giving unnecessary injections instead of standing up for what is right. The babies and children are terribly spoilt and it is almost impossible to admit a child of six to seven years of age without its mother. The nurses' work is made very difficult by the numerous relatives, and Chinese curiosity is insatiable, they pry and stare with no regard for privacy and no place seems inaccessible to them.

The people here are more primitive than those in Hankow; they are really filthy, even the rich. Opium smoking is very common and perhaps almost half the population take opium in some form, even giving it to children. In addition, Chinese Medicine is such that patients go from one doctor to another collecting prescriptions until they are either better, or die. They regard our medicine in the same way, and often attend our hospital and the Catholic hospital at the same time, taking native medicine as well. If we do not cure them with one dose then they go somewhere else instead; for instance, very few patients ever attend more than three or four N.A.B's for syphilis. Surgery is still very suspect and one does not run risks. I had a patient with a large goitre die at operation and because I did cardiac massage it was thought I had removed her heart and that is why she died! We know that these are the reasons why we have come to China and are learning to bear with them.

The money situation is most unstable with a silver dollar now worth twenty four thousand paper dollars - a jump from five hundred in three weeks. Winnie as hospital accountant finds it a very complicated business.

6am April 29th 1949 - letter from Chaotung.

Frank:-

Dear Grandparents, Great Aunts, All,

Rosemary Ann was born yesterday morning at 11.50am. She is a perfect little baby, quite strong though only 6 lbs. in weight. Winnie is splendid. The baby was nearly a week in coming, but Winnie was up and working again until Wednesday evening.

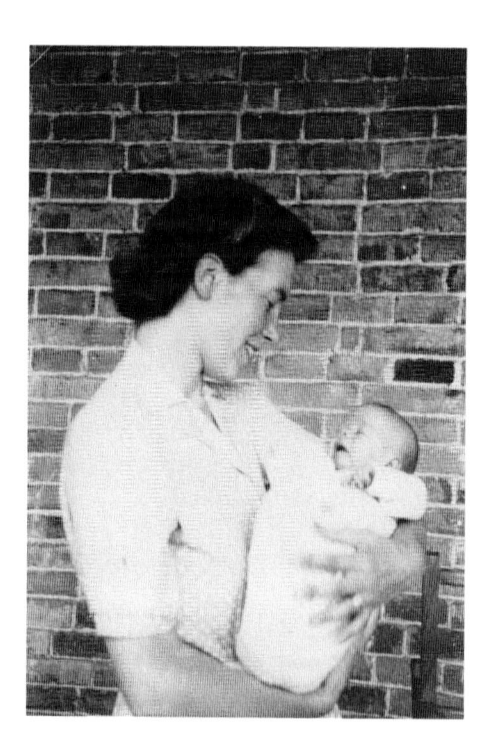

All the nurses were quite worried the baby was so long coming but now they are all excited just as we are. Winnie has received some lovely flowers and sweet peas and many pretty little dresses.

We sent a cable to you yesterday - I hope it arrives safely. We are sorry so few of our letters are getting home. We have been waiting a fortnight now for the special 'plane to bring us money and supplies, and holding up letters to put on the 'plane because there are no stamps purchasable in Chaotung Post Office now. Letters have started to come through to us again quite regularly and Journals too. Winnie loves to receive Miss Featherstone's 'Woman's Weekly' and Mummy's 'Woman's Journal'. I am enclosing a letter to Dorothy Reece, which will tell you about last week.

Two days ago there were two thousand bandits twenty miles north west of the city, but they did not worry us, all our work goes on as usual.

Our garden is now looking very nice. The strawberry beds have been arranged and we have planted some chrysanthemums. Some beautiful delphiniums, antirrhinums, flax, cornflowers, marigolds and wallflowers are in bloom now. The weather is very changeable; heavy showers, bright sunshine, then cold mountain wind. The cuckoo has arrived, though it is called 'Bough Goo' bird - meaning maize bird - the idea being that the bird is saying it is time to plant the 'Bough Goo'.

The plane is now supposed to be arriving at noon today but, as it is raining heavily now, I don't know whether once again it will have to be put off. Hospital salaries are in arrears so I hope it comes.
Lots of love from us all.
F, W & Rosemary.

May 12th May 1949 - letter from Chaotung.

Winnie:-

Well, here I am at last writing a letter, which I said I would do a week ago at least. It's amazing how quickly the days have passed since Rosemary was born. She is fourteen days old today. She is a little darling and I'm sure you will love her. Frank is going to take some photos of her in a few days and if post gets easier we hope to send you some.

The general China situation gets worse day by day, the 'News' last night said the Communists were within twenty miles of Hankow and something about their having captured Changsha. The trouble with the British boats on the Yangtze is not too good either. Just lately we have been able to hear the news every night but now our battery is fairly low so we shall have to do without for a while.

May 12th May 1949 - letter from Chaotung to Frank's brother, John.

> *Frank:-*
>
> *Now, Dr. Wang is a real missionary doctor here with a sense of vocation. He could have obtained a first class job in a big hospital quite easily with his ability; also, his parents opposed his coming here. Since being here his father has died and when this happens in China the eldest son is expected to return home and look after all the affairs of the whole family but Dr. Wang has stayed on. His salary is sixty pounds sterling a year. His wife is very lonely in this strange place with a strange dialect. Dr. Wang continues to give all he has to the medical work and religious life of the hospital. What he needs more than anything are good medical books, which, even if he could afford them, are just unobtainable here. Until one lives here it is hard to imagine just how isolated and inaccessible we are now that the Communists have cut off so much of China.*

Chaotung Hospital staff on 29th May 1949

Starting 4th person from left front row: Frank, Winnie, Dr Nieh (Physician and Hospital Superintendent), Miss Ma (Matron), Win Sanderson (nurse), Dr Wong (recruited in Hankow).

JUNE 1949 - FINAL WEEKS

Long before we set foot in China in 1947 Mao Tse-Tung's army were working their way across the north of the country. News of his movements made very little impact on the general public in England. Indeed I think we were all too busy recovering from the effects of the Second World War to pay much attention to countries on the other side of the world. Therefore, although rumours were circulating in Hankow whilst we were there, that Mao's troops were moving south ever closer to Hankow, nobody appeared too worried about it.

Later in 1948 when we were in Chaotung, we were so far away that news arrived quite slowly, and local disturbances did not arouse undue concern in this remote area, because they were usually caused by 'bandits'. However, although any disruption was a good excuse for lawless behaviour, the trouble at that time was not purely that of local bandits. Not long after Rosemary was born, by mid-May 1949, Mao Tse-Tung had taken over a large area of Central and Eastern China and proclaimed the People's Republic of China. The evidence of political uprising and its real dangers could not be ignored.

Frank and I were the latest addition to the missionary group in Yunnan and as such had no say in matters concerning what action, if any, should be taken if China's political situation changed. Our more senior colleagues kept in constant touch with Kunming and eventually received a message from the British High Commissioner to the effect that, 'all women and children should be evacuated from Chaotung as soon as possible'. This prompted a flurry of activity.

May 27th 1949 - letter from Chaotung to Frank's parents.

Frank:-

I am writing first a short note in order to catch the plane going to Kunming and will write more fully later. In accordance with instructions to reduce staff to a minimum and evacuate all women and children.

Winnie and Rosemary are leaving Chaotung by plane on June the first for Hong Kong and then to fly almost immediately to England (four days journey). One of our nurses is going with Winnie to help with the baby.

I am staying on, probably, and will leave six months later to join Winnie at home.

There are several places where Winnie and baby may be able to stay temporarily - Ockbrook with Mrs. Hill, at Worthing or Bathampton, whichever is best. It would probably be nice for Winnie to spend a little time at each. For the first month Winnie will need thorough rest and holiday, quite unbothered by any business questions and arrangements - she is badly in need of this.

If possible it would be very much best if Winnie could be met by car and taken wherever she is going to stay, so that the journey can be as restful as possible.

There is nothing in the present situation to cause you any worry or anxiety. It is just a preliminary precautionary measure so that complete evacuation, if it becomes necessary later, will be simplified.
With all our love and trust in your love to understand,
Frank.

On June 1st 1949, a group of about twenty women and children, including Rosemary and me, clambered into the Lutheran Mission plane, 'St. Paul', a small twin engine prop plane, for the journey to Kunming.

There were no seats inside the plane. I remember sitting on the floor, side by side with the others, surrounded by luggage and Rosemary in her carrycot, our legs outstretched and our backs resting against the side of the plane. The luggage allowance was strictly limited to sixty pounds per passenger, with no extra for a baby. I found that, after packing nappies and clothes for Rosemary, my personal clothing had to be restricted to two summer weight dresses, a couple of pairs of pyjamas, a few undies and essential toiletries. All other accessories were stuffed under Rosemary in her carrycot. Fortunately, the distance between Chaotung and Kunming was only three hundred miles, so the flight time was relatively short.

The flight was actually quite an endurance test, being in a Dakota and without any air pressure adjustment. The plane followed a route between the peaks of the mountains, keeping as low an altitude as possible. Even so it was quite bumpy.

On landing in Kunming we were immediately transported to the homes of various missionary colleagues. There was quite a lot of confusion about whether we should be sent to India or back to England. Mission House in London thought that we could stay in Calcutta for a short time, and then return to China once the political upheaval settled down. They had no idea of the seriousness of the situation in China. On the other hand, our colleagues on the field knew very well that Mao Tse-Tung would not tolerate the presence of Christian missionaries working in his country. Eventually, it was agreed that we should go to Calcutta and remain there while Mission House finally came to a decision. Meanwhile, I collected Rosemary's birth certificate and obtained a fresh photograph, which included Rosemary so that she could be entered on my passport.

Owing to the ever-changing plans, Rosemary's feeding times were greatly upset. We were concerned that during the journey back to England it might be necessary to supplement her feeding, and we endeavoured to make provision for this before departing for Calcutta. We provided ourselves with a primus stove, feeding bottles and so on, and were fortunate enough to obtain a very small supply of 'Klin' baby milk. I look back in horror to think that I actually flew from Kunming to Calcutta with a primus stove in my luggage.

June 2nd 1949 - letter from Winnie to Frank written in Kunming.

Winnie:-

The first night we were all so tired that we did not sleep well and yesterday we spent doing very little except filling in forms for the China National Airways trip to India tomorrow. We are all going and they think that the plane comes down for the night at Rangoon and goes on to Calcutta on Monday.

I have Rosemary's birth certificate. The Consul had it ready, but not posted. Also, for the air trip tomorrow we had to have Passport photos. I have had another one taken with the baby, this time Alison Kendall's doll wrapped up in a blanket!

We had a lovely flight over 'the hump' to Rangoon, although quite a few folks were sick. I felt fine all the way, but there were no big 'drops' such as we experienced when flying from Hankow.

My sixty pounds of luggage has now been weighed and taken to the airfield. We are off at twelve noon tomorrow. The rest of our party are to go up to the hills in India until their passages are booked. Mu says Greg (the nurse allocated to assist me in looking after Rosemary) and I are booked to leave Calcutta on the 10th June, we are hoping the Klin will last as we cannot buy any more of the things we wanted here. No cottonseed oil, no Lactogol and no Cow and Gate. Better luck in Calcutta.

Letter continued in Rangoon

It is now Whitsunday night and we are in the Strand Hotel, Rangoon. We left Kunming this afternoon at two o'clock and had a wonderful trip arriving in Rangoon, six o'clock (four-thirty p.m their time). Everyone has been so kind and made every effort to get us off. No trouble with Customs. We were given a cup of tea at the airport here and then taken to Rangoon in a bus.

The airport is a three quarter of an hour drive from the hotel. 'The Strand' has about four hundred rooms and is just super. Dinner was soup, fish, mutton, peas and potatoes, followed by blanc-mange, coffee and banana ices. About fifty Burmese waiters served us, walking around in snow-white suits, and little black hats. Fans were going everywhere. Greg and I are sharing a room. We have a fan, a bedside lamp and flask of cold water beside each bed; a mosquito net each, our own lavatory and bathroom, a writing desk and balcony - just like a film set.

Must close now as we have to be up at five o'clock to feed baby and get ready for breakfast at six o'clock. We should leave the airport at eight o'clock. Tomorrow we shall be in Calcutta. Mu has booked for Greg and me on a plane leaving Calcutta on the tenth and thinks we should arrive in England next Sunday.
(In the event we all travelled back together to England.)

Tuesday 8:15 a.m. June 7th 1949 - letter from Calcutta.
Winnie:-
We are in Calcutta awaiting breakfast. Oh my, it is hot, one just drips with perspiration all the time. Now, more details of Rangoon - the sky was clear for most of the flight from Kunming, after passing over mile upon mile of mountains we suddenly dropped down over the flat land about half an hour before landing. The Monsoon must have begun. There were miles of flooded rice fields - water, water everywhere. In addition to the rice-fields there were stretches of woodland, making a beautiful and luxurious emerald green pattern. Rangoon itself was a very well kept, up-to-date city, and we wish that we could have seen more of it. Once again, we had a smooth flight and a wonderful view, especially of the coastline of Burma.

Obviously I had not told Frank about the extremely bumpy flight over the 'hump' from Kunming to Rangoon. Nor had I mentioned the very cramped conditions we experienced on the plane from Chaotung to Kunming, when we sat facing one another on very low canvas seats, rather like paratroopers. I guess I did not wish to worry him with my discomforts and difficulties when he had plenty to contend with in Chaotung.

Arrived in Calcutta at eleven o'clock Rangoon time where we had a long wait getting through Customs and a longer bus ride into the City. It is boiling hot in the heat of the day and poor little Rosemary was pouring with perspiration. She did not sleep very well and we gave her fluids, as much as she would take. The last two nights she has woken up and taken three ounces of water, but she is fine.

After Customs yesterday, we finally arrived at the Methodist Church at two in the afternoon (Calcutta time from now on), where a Mrs Remfrey took charge of Greg and me. Here we are in a lovely flat, with fans in every room, a separate bathroom, and lots of very smart servants. We are just about to have breakfast, then Mrs Remfrey will take us to Cook's Travel to enquire about our next trip. If possible I will post this today and give you more news later.

<u>Wednesday June 8th 1949</u> - letter from Calcutta.

Winnie:-

Poor darling, your letter did not get posted after all - better luck next time. We are having a lovely time here. Mr and Mrs Remfrey are full of kindness and have thought of everything. Mrs Remfrey is very quiet and gentle and a real lady; she is sweet about the baby. They had three children but, sadly, for some unknown reason none survived. This morning Greg stayed in whilst Mrs Remfrey and I went shopping. Imagine my surprise when I had chosen a set of nylon undies and a set of cotton ones, all hand embroidered, altogether costing about thirty rupees (£2.10s.0d.), when Mrs Remfrey insisted on giving them to me as a present; and later on she also bought me a dress length of cotton material - yellow/black design on a white-cream background - rather attractive. She is a sweet soul. Perhaps, a little later on, you might be able to find a moment to write them a wee note of thanks for all the care and kindness they are showing me.

Do you know, this afternoon, we all had to be re-vaccinated and have another Cholera injection, just because your certificates are not on form number so and so.

My arm does hurt. I don't know what will happen about Rosemary as Charles says the Air Office say that any baby over one day old has to be done. We shall see.

Latest News - All except the Steel family expect to fly home, leaving Calcutta at nine-fifteen on Saturday and arriving at London Airport on Sunday at nine p.m. English time, 12th of June. What will Mission House say?

Did I tell you that we have started baby on Ostermilk, as Cow and Gate is not available. She has taken it for two days now and seems to be OK. Today, poor wee thing, she has been somewhat fretful. She has quite a bit of prickly heat, so have I, and I do sympathise with her.

I saw in 'The Statesman' this morning, Thursday, 'Communist Forces advancing towards Canton.' I was going to go to the post with this, but baby has not settled down. Mrs Remfrey is taking us to the pictures this afternoon to see 'The Blue Lagoon', and tomorrow evening, I have been invited to dinner by a Mrs Gibson with whom Eleanor is staying. Rosemary is invited as well. Mrs Gibson has some films of Calcutta.

Will really post this now my beloved. Take care of yourself and if you cannot find time to write very often please don't worry, I shall know and understand, I know God will keep you in his care.
Your loving wife, Winnie.
Rosemary sends Wa-a-a-a- and says, 'Oh dear, it is hot!'

The temperature was about 104°F and very humid as the Monsoon had just begun.

Thursday June 9th 1949 - letter from Calcutta.
Winnie:-
Still no letter sent. Went to the Post Office this morning and they said they were not selling stamps until between four and five pm so will go along later. We are

having a cool shower here every afternoon. All the trees and flowers are looking fresh and the grass is a most gorgeous, fresh, emerald green. The humidity though, is as bad as Hankow. I am smothered with prickly heat and so is Rosemary. She was restless and crying all morning but has slept soundly all the afternoon so far.

Have just been told that we can only take sixty-six pounds of baggage and no hand baggage apart from handbag. I get no allowance for Rosemary regardless of the fact that we have to pay ten percent of adult fare for her and she doesn't get a seat. Pan-American Airways certainly seem sticky about details. How different from China.

There were no more letters for a few days because we were flying back to England.

June 15th 1949 - letter from Bathampton.

Winnie:-

Here I am at last, sitting in the dining room at nine fifteen on the morning of 15th June. Oh, dearest, how I wish you could be here to share the joy with us all. Everybody is so anxious to see the baby, Aunt Irene has already asked me whether she can give us a pram, many people have offered to lend cots and baby clothes. Mr. Payne says, 'They're all talking so much about the baby that nobody thinks about the mother.'

We arrived in England on Monday afternoon. I will write you details of the journey later as Mummy says a post is going out very shortly and I want this to get to you as soon as possible. Yesterday I arrived in Bath and everybody is just wonderful. Have quite a few things to do right now as I have had a late breakfast. The weather is just lovely at the moment. Rosemary is out in the garden. Zettie came in a little while ago to see baby and watch her have a bath. I'm sure she is going to get terribly spoilt.

Lots more news to follow.

In the garden in Bathampton
Winnie, Rosemary,
Nellie Tovey (Frank's mother),
John (Frank's brother) and
'Scottie' the dog.

(The dog is sitting in a basket attached to the front of the pram.)

June 15th and 16th 1949 - extract from letter from Bathampton to Frank.

Winnie:-

Now, for details of the rest of our journey home. As you know, we flew by Pan-American Airways - supposed to leave Calcutta, 9:15 p.m., to be in London and 9:15 a.m. the next day. To begin with, we were allowed only 66lbs of baggage and no extra for the baby and less hand baggage than the Chinese allowance. So, I had to leave the Primus, saucepan and two empty cases behind with Mrs Remfrey. She will see if some of the up-country missionaries would like them in India.

The plane left Calcutta in good time and we had a smooth trip to New Delhi, arriving at one o'clock in the morning. At each airport all passengers have to leave the plane because of the danger of fire whilst refuelling. They served a small meal in the restaurant, then we received word that an engine was faulty and we should have to wait awhile. We waited until two o'clock in the afternoon and it was hot; absolutely baking, poor Rosemary just cried and cried with the heat and all the others were miserable with loss of sleep.

I remember pacing gently up and down across the Waiting Hall trying to comfort Rosemary. After a while a kind Indian Ayah came over and offered to share the nursing. She took Rosemary over for an hour so that I could rest. So kind, she would not take a tip.

Finally we were off at two-thirty and landed at Karachi after three to four hours flying. Here we had another meal, our passports were examined and we were off again in about an hour, after an engine check.

The next stretch was an eight hour flight and we all slept, came down at Damascus at two in the morning. Had breakfast and were told there was 'more engine trouble'. We waited again until 4am, then set off just as dawn was breaking. This time we did ten and a half flying hours and had a most wonderful view of the Italian Alps, with snow capped mountains, sweeping glaciers and some lovely lakes, all seen in brilliant sunshine. We reached Brussels at two-thirty in the afternoon, their time, and arrived in England (Heathrow) at five o'clock GMT.

There was nobody to meet us except Mrs Kendall's parents. We had tea, then the airfield bus took us into Town somewhere, where Miss Porter and the Rev Rattenbury (from Mission House) met us. They told us (Greg and me) where to go for the night and it was all over. I telephoned Daddy later in the evening and we arranged for me to catch the eleven fifteen train next day, arriving Bath at one o'clock. This I did and here we are.

Mummy said that John went home especially, after my cable, and stayed up until two o'clock one morning trying to persuade Daddy to let someone come and meet me, with no luck. However, I am none the worse apart from the terrible tiredness. It makes me feel I want to run away from everything, even baby. I am writing to ask Mother to come and see me as soon as possible, maybe that will help.

This seems to be an appropriate place for a few words of explanation regarding some of the remarks made in the letter on the previous page. The actual flying time from Calcutta to Heathrow was twenty hours, to which seventeen hours should be added for time spent waiting for engine repairs in Delhi, Karachi and Damascus airports. Altogether the journey took thirty-seven hours and we were all extremely exhausted. The fact that I knew none of the Methodist Mission House staff accounted for my forlorn feeling on arrival at Heathrow; nor was I familiar with London. During the protracted flight the supply of 'safe' drinking water on board the aeroplane ran out, making it extremely difficult to cope with feeding Rosemary. My supply of breast milk all but dried up and, as you will realise, I was unable to make up any supplementary feeds without water. Neither Brussels nor Heathrow held any stock of baby milk.

That first night in England was altogether pretty traumatic. Rosemary was obviously hungry. Whilst the plane was airborne she had slept solidly, but immediately we touched down she started crying fretfully. Once we reached the hotel (I have no idea which one) I dashed out to an all-night chemist shop. When I asked for a tin of milk powder for a baby the Assistant said, 'Where is your Ration Book? I can't sell you any without it.' Whereupon I burst into tears and told him that I did not possess the Ration Book, having just arrived in the country by plane late in the afternoon. He was quite sympathetic and asked whether I could produce proof of this fact. At that time the airline would hand out a 'flight card' to each passenger. These cards were stamped with the date and time of flight, and one was able to record places of interest over which the plane flew during the course of the journey. Fortunately, I had my 'flight card' in my handbag. I handed it over to the Assistant and, with no more ado, he bent down and brought out a tin of Cow and Gate milk powder from under the counter. My one and only black market purchase, I think. Armed with this tin I returned to the hotel bedroom and stood looking at the tap wondering whether it was safe to give Rosemary milk made up with unboiled tap water. (In China, we had to boil all our drinking water.) It was very late at night and no room service available. Courageously, I made up an eight-ounce bottle of milk and was astonished when Rosemary drank every drop in record time and dropped off into a deep sleep. Three hours later she awoke again and once more I offered her another bottle of milk.

More travel and disruption of routine followed, and you will realise, from my letters to Frank, that many months were to pass before Rosemary began to recover from the great upheavals that had taken place during the first six weeks of her life.

A newspaper cutting announcing Winnie and Rosemary's safe arrival from China.

Evacuated from China

Mrs. Tovey, the wife of Dr. Frank Tovey, F.R.C.S., arrived in England by air from China on Monday last with her infant daughter of seven weeks. She is for the present staying with Mr. and Mrs. Ernest Tovey, at Bathampton, Bath.

On the instructions of the British Consul, all women and children have been evacuated from S.W. China. Leaving Chaotung on June 2, Mrs. Tovey was first of all flown to Kunming. From there the next stage of the journey was to Rangoon and Calcutta. Leaving Calcutta by Pan-American Airways on June 11, the party of 24 women and children was delayed at Damascus because of engine trouble, finally arriving in London on Monday, approximately a day late.

Dr. Frank Tovey is remaining in S.W. China in charge of the Methodist Hospital at Chaotung.

* *

June 16th 1949 - letter from Bathampton.

Winnie:-

It is five-thirty in the morning and I have just woken from a twelve-hour sleep without a break, the first one I've had for ages. Dearest, I am afraid I have rather disgraced myself but I have been absolutely dead tired ever since we left Chaotung and, the continual loss of sleep, the heat and insufficient food to keep going on properly throughout the journey made me more tired than ever. I reached Bath at one o'clock on Tuesday, then fed baby, had lunch, a short rest, fed baby, tea, then washed three days' collection of nappies, fed baby. John came, had supper and we got to bed about half past ten. I was up again at three and five-thirty.

Wednesday, I had late breakfast at eight-thirty, then, as I said earlier, Zettie came to watch Rosemary have her bath. Later I did some ironing, and after lunch Mummy and I went to rest out in the sun but, unfortunately, I got none at all as baby was crying nearly all day with tummy ache. (We have had to change the type of milk again). Auntie May came at five o'clock, just as Mummy had decided to go for some Dil water. Off went Mummy saying to me, 'You get tea'. Auntie May had the sweetest little toy for Rosemary and, after giving me this, she said, 'You look tired. Do let me get the tea. You go and rest for a while.' Those few words just unwound me; I went into the bedroom and just wept and wept. When Mummy came back she gave me a cup of tea and two tablets and sent me to bed. She kept baby all night and had very little sleep indeed as Rosemary took two hours over one feed then, after two hours woke again, fed, slept for an hour and is now awake again.

Oh, how I long for quiet and peace for baby and me. How I should manage with everything to do for myself I do not know, but everybody is so anxious to see the baby that she gets too many disturbances and too much attention to settle down well. In addition, I have almost completely run out of breast milk, and our stock of Ostermilk ran out on the flight from Calcutta so that she has had to go back to Klin for two or thee feeds. All I could buy without a Ration Book in London was Cow and Gate and since being in Bathampton Rosemary has been sick after each feed and has had some colicky pain. She is taking much more than she should for her weight and not enough for her age. We are going to the Baby Clinic in Bath tomorrow.

At that time baby milk preparations were only obtainable from a Baby Clinic. The baby was weighed and a monthly allocation of milk powder calculated according to the weight of the baby. In Rosemary's case this meant that, because she was underweight for her age, she was never granted a sufficient quantity to satisfy her hunger. Also, in 1949, it was considered inadvisable to feed babies on complementary foods until they were 12lbs or more in weight.

One other inconvenience was that I had arrived home with no money and to begin with Mission House did not send any. Imagine my difficulty having to ask Frank's father for a small amount for personal necessities. He could not understand why I needed money as we were living in his home. I hardly knew Frank's parents as we set sail so soon after being married and had no idea that Frank had been required to keep an account of all his expenditure, down to the last penny, during the whole of his student life. What a lot I had to learn.

In my home circumstances my brother Arthur and I had been obliged to contribute to the family budget from the age of fourteen, first of all by doing Saturday work, then, as soon as our school days ended, we obtained a full time job and contributed a specified amount from our earnings towards our 'keep'.

Rosemary continued to be very unsettled and was not gaining weight, which worried me. After a week or so in Bathampton I moved up to Ockbrook. There I was able to rent a flat on the Moravian Settlement. We were blessed with four or five weeks of glorious summer weather and spent nearly every day sitting out in the peaceful school garden, soaking up the sun. With the help and encouragement of friends I dared to supplement Rosemary's diet with solids, (milk alone never seemed to satisfy her), and she flourished. She was a bonny six-month-old when Frank joined us in the October.

June 7th 1949 letter from Chaotung to Bathampton.

Frank:-

Darling, here we have decided to keep all three houses on the compound open. I am sleeping in this house and using the study. George and Ken come here to feed and use the sitting room. Everyone congregates in here for the evening news. George and Ken are sleeping in the North house and Kuan's wife is looking after them. Ken is keeping his horse boy to look at after the Stone Gateway horses and to carry water.

We have had some trouble with our servants and Cheng Hsin Te has been most upset. He was first made to tell us that unless we kept on all the servants belonging to the house they would go on strike. Then, when we made it clear that we laid down conditions and not them, and said that we could afford to keep all except the old man, more trouble started. Our idea was to ask Ert and the Lung Tzu to carry water between them. The old man's son (Stone's boy) came up and said quite politely, but definitely, that he would beat up anyone who took his father's job.

Ken is getting a constant stream of visitors all day long and remains wonderfully patient. My, he gets some trying people; 'Hallelujah' trying to swindle him; the people who brought goods down on the second plane trying to get out of paying, and so on.

We had a wonderfully blind, ridiculous wire from London saying delay evacuation and send mothers to wait in Hong Kong and concentrate rest of personnel in Chaotung and Kunming sending all but language students to live at Kunming. Is any more comment needed?

Yesterday they were arranging to carry a rain dragon through the town in a plea for rain, but now I don't know whether that will be necessary. Last night, we had a heavy rain and thunderstorm. George says the rain dragon is held aloft on poles, each man carrying a section. It is covered with green rushes and the men are constantly sprinkled with water. A huo p'an is also carried with rushes over the fire, the significance of this is uncertain.

I am taking the junior nurses' English Class now on Tuesday and Wednesday mornings and looking forward to having some fun out of it.

Yesterday evenings' 'Eastern News' said the Kunming Consul had ordered all non-essential people to leave Yunnan because of unrest due to the Peoples' Army. We are waiting to see how this affects us. We have an epidemic of measles in the town and barracks, with crowds of cases, so it is a good thing Rosemary has left. Yesterday afternoon in outpatients were two cases of smallpox.

June 12th 1949 - letter from Chaotung.

Frank:-

I wish I knew where you are now - on the plane, in Calcutta, or at home - and how you and baby are getting on. I am feeling very cross with myself; I must have picked up amoebic dysentery at one of the Chinese feasts and since last Tuesday I have had to stay in bed. My great hope is that you haven't got the same thing.

Ken and Edna have gone out to Stone Gateway for the weekend. It has really begun to rain in earnest now, so I hope they are not having too wet a time. Joan still comes in every night for the 'news' and cocoa before going to bed. George is now living on the compound, silent and witty, but good company. Win hasn't moved yet and gives me my nightly Emetine. Last night we had a pleasant time with the gramophone and George is going to bring out some of Vernon's records for tonight. We are very much living in together as one community now.

The China News is very contradictory still. One night we hear of Communists in Kwantung on the way to Canton and another night they haven't yet entered Changsha. Sometimes it is reported that they definitely mean to attack Hong Kong and other times that the Communists are anxious to maintain friendly relations.

We are all feeling that our stay here may be shorter than we first thought. I have got the hospital accounts up-to-date and am going to instruct Dr. Nieh and Dr Wang in the book keeping, stores etc, in case they are unexpectedly left alone. Dr Wang is very upset at the possibility that we may have to go, especially because he came all this way in order to work with me. I have asked him if he would like to come weekly again for tuition and have suggested that we do Monday antenatal clinics together so that he can have some training in midwifery too. I'm strongly trying to persuade Dr. Nieh to have only one three-hour Out Patient Department session a day if we have to leave the hospital. The hospital is still full in spite of the rain and Win is kept very busy.

My darling, my thoughts are with you both continually and I miss you in so many ways, more than I can say. I'm afraid that, with your going, I feel I don't really belong here but ought to be where you are and just long for the time when we shall be together again. Till then we must do all we can to hold the situation here and prepare for handing it over. We here have become very dependent upon one another and each day we all unconsciously make an effort to meet together, just for company.

God keep you safe my darling and give you His peace and joy.
My love to Mummy, Daddy, John, Aunties and Mother,
Forever, your loving Frank.

July 10th 1949 - letter from Mr. & Mrs. Remfrey, Calcutta, to Frank's parents in Bathampton.

Dear Mr and Mrs Tovey

Thank you very much indeed for your kind letter of the 26th June, which my husband and I were so pleased to receive. It was a great pleasure to us to be able to offer hospitality to your daughter-in-law and her little babe during the week they spent in Calcutta on their way home from China, and we were so glad to hear of their safe arrival in England, although sorry that the plane was delayed for twenty-four hours. However, this may have made the journey a little less tiring, for flying for many hours continuously becomes very fatiguing and one longs for the roar of the engines to cease for awhile.

It was very wonderful how air passages were procured for these travellers from China so quickly, and we were very glad indeed that Mrs Frank Tovey had kind Sister Gregory to accompany her on the journey, and to give her such loving and capable help with Rosemary. It was a tremendous undertaking with a little six-week-old baby; but we are so thankful and glad that it was accomplished safely. We had a letter from Miss Gregory too, and were so glad to hear of her safe arrival at her own home, visiting London on her way. She did not actually say so, but we hope that she was able to travel down to Bath with Mrs Frank and the baby, where you were there to meet them and give them welcome.

Here in India, now we are in the Monsoon, but as the rains have not really broken properly yet, it is very steamy, a condition that many people find extremely trying.

Kindest regards and every good wish

Irene Remfrey.

Frank's last few weeks in Chaotung and journey home - 1949

There was something very sad and final watching the Lutheran plane, St. Paul, as it took off from the Chaotung Airstrip with Winnie and Rosemary, plus the other wives and children on board. Life suddenly became very empty.

Dr Nieh was having to take longer and longer periods of time away from the hospital meeting people in the town; there was no doubt about his personal concern for his future, being a Nosu and belonging to a family of landlords. The surgical work kept us busy and this meant Dr Wang was able to do increasingly more surgery. He would come of an evening for tutorials at least twice a week. Our weekly Missionary Fellowship meetings continued and were of great help to us all.

Conflicting news continued to arrive about the fate of the churches and of missionaries in Communist occupied areas. Although some reported little opposition, apart from restriction of movement, other reports were much more unfavourable. Ken and I remained definite that we wished to leave before any takeover and, in any case, within six months, although other colleagues were less doubtful about staying and inclined to await events.

On July 7, 1949, a telegram came from Mission House:-

'Missionaries all churches continuing after changeover. Permanent difficulty communications are not expected. Urge this amelioration position will enable you holdover.'

During the week of July 23rd, however, one of the senior Chinese pastors in Chaotung, met with us and said that the continued presence of missionaries would be an embarrassment to the Church.

We sent a telegram accordingly to Kunming:-

'Information recently received raises question advisability staying Chaotung takeover. Local Church strongly advise total evacuation before takeover. Do you advise remaining staff leave with Ken and Frank?'

By this time we had been informed that Ken and I would be flown out by a commercial plane on or about August 5th. This was later changed to August 13th and we were told that two berths had been booked on the P&O ship 'Canton' for September 30th. However, It proved that the only available aeroplane was too large to land on the airstrip in Chaotung.

Some of us took advantage of the delay in flights to spend a long weekend in Stone Gateway. We saw a number of patients and visited the leprosy colony. This, with other buildings, had been badly damaged by the series of earthquakes. We visited a crude, papermaking factory, using pulped bamboo and an earthen kiln.

On August 15th, when I was in outpatients, a message came asking me to go to the town to receive a phone call from Kunming. The call was very faint and difficult to understand, having been routed via Kweiyang to Chungking, thence to Libing, many miles to the north, and onwards to Chaotung. The caller said that the St Paul (Lutheran Mission plane) would be arriving for us on Wednesday August 24th and that we should proceed the next day to Hong Kong to sail on the 'Corfu' for Tilbury on September 2nd.

The next few days were ones of great activity. First of all the hospital accounts had to be balanced. Silver dollars, gold bars, bales of cloth, sugar and salt, all required conversion into current value, and in the end I was fifty four dollars out when I handed them over.

To pay for the plane we offered a payload of two thousand pounds in weight to a commercial firm 'on the street', who sold it in lots to various customers.

On Wednesday, August 24th, we traipsed the three miles down to the airstrip, with coolies carrying our packing cases and baggage slung on carrying poles. Amongst other items we took the hospital scales to enable us to check the weight of the two thousand pound payload. We sat all day on the edge of the airfield and no plane came. A tyre had punctured in Kunming, but we did not know this at the time, so back we went, luggage and all, to the hospital.

The next day we reassembled, but this time although the plane flew over it could not land because of cloud. We assembled again on the Friday but nothing happened. On each of these occasions we reweighed the payload to make sure that nothing had been added.

On Saturday, August 27th, it was a beautiful day. This time we decided to trust the Chinese payload and we did not take the hospital weighing scales. During the afternoon, at about three o'clock, the plane suddenly appeared at a low level coming silently round the mountain. It landed perfectly and taxied up towards us. The two pilots were Germans. That day they had started from Hong Kong, flown to Kweiling, thence to Chungking and on to Chaotung. After leaving us at Kunming they had to go to Liehang. They flew by contact, picking up landmarks as they went.

They informed us that we had to cut our payload by six hundred pounds and that started a virtual fight, with everyone trying to get their payload of freight on board. The An Chuan Yuen had provided a guard each day, but there was not much that they could do. We had great difficulty in keeping the crowd clear when the aeroplane's door was closed, and I fear that some fingers must have been crushed. When we came to take off, the pilots realised that the plane was overloaded. By not bringing the scales we had given the Chinese an opportunity to pack more silver dollars and gold in their payload. The plane became airborne just at the end of the runway, and we all let out a huge sigh of relief.

Understandably, the pilots were quite angry with us for our carelessness. Later we were forgiven when they understood our predicament. They were both stateless, with no passports. They had families in Canton and wanted to move to Hong Kong, but, without passports, could not do so. An appeal was being organised on their behalf by the Lutheran Mission. We arrived in Kunming at four thirty.

On Tuesday, August 30th, Ken and I were part of a party that boarded the Skymaster flight in Kunming, on its route from Calcutta to Hong Kong.

In Hong Kong we stayed once again at the Methodist Seamen's Mission. For the next two days we were kept busy arranging the shipping of the baggage we brought with us.

We boarded the 'Corfu' on Friday, September 2nd, and on Saturday the 3rd of September the Yunnan revolution was reported. It was not clear at first who had rebelled, but in fact it was virtually a bloodless takeover by the Communist Army. We had escaped by four days.

Ken Parsons and I shared a cabin. The voyage home was enjoyable, though constantly tinged by the anxiety to be home with Winnie and Rosemary. At Singapore we were entertained by ex-nurse Rainer, one of the first Chaotung nurses who was married to the Singapore manager of May & Baker. In Penang we spent a happy day with Ban it Chiu, his wife Wendy, and their three-year old son, Michael. There we visited, amongst other places, the famous snake temple.

The journey ended on October 3rd in Tilbury where the boat train was waiting to take us into London. Our crates were left in charge of Cooks, and as soon as possible, I caught the train at St. Pancras to be met, to our great joy, by Winnie at Derby Station. A quick bus journey took us to Ockbrook to be reunited with baby Rosemary.

Back in England - 1949 to 1951

Rosemary and I stayed in Bathampton for a couple of weeks immediately after our arrival in England and then moved to Ockbrook where we resided in the Moravian Settlement throughout the summer. This proved to be a great blessing, as it was a haven of peace and tranquillity, where we were able to recover from the tremendous upheavals of the previous few months.

The Moravian Settlement in Ockbrook was established in 1799, and in 1949 it was one of three or four such Settlements still in existence in England. It was surrounded by its own boundaries, creating the atmosphere of a small, self-contained village. On one day in each year, the road running through the old Settlement was closed to through traffic for twenty-four hours in order to maintain right of ownership. Within the Settlement the church remained the pivotal point. Next to it stood the school, and around these two main buildings there were various groups of houses, one row for married couples, one for single 'brethren' and one for single 'sisters'.

Ockbrook School was ideally situated to provide just what we required. The summer vacation was about to begin and I was offered the use of a flat within the school buildings for a peppercorn rent. In addition to this, I was given permission to make use of the school gardens for relaxation. The adjacent village of Ockbrook had its own general grocery store, a butcher's shop and a post office. We were surrounded by lots of kind friends and neighbours.

The weather was absolutely gorgeous, with weeks of warm, sunny days. I was extremely grateful for this, being very short of clothing. As mentioned in my earlier letters, on leaving Chaotung our luggage allowance was extremely limited. After packing together all the nappies and necessary articles needed for a five week old baby there was just enough leeway to enable me to take one change of clothing for myself.

Towards the end of September I left the school flat and moved into another flat on the Settlement, which was set apart for the use of Missionaries during their furlough. This is where Frank joined us when he came home from Chaotung early in October 1949.

Frank and Winnie
October 1949.

Immediately after Frank's arrival we needed to give our minds to deciding our way forward. Mission House informed us that there was no suitable vacancy for a surgeon overseas for the time being, so it was decided that he should seek a post in the United Kingdom. At that time he had only fulfilled two years of his five-year contract with the Methodist Missionary Society.

Frank was extremely fortunate in that, after a short period of leave, he obtained a post as Surgical Registrar in Southmead Hospital, Bristol. Having spent the whole of his medical training years in Bristol before going to China he was already familiar with the hospitals and had many friends amongst the medical fraternity. However, after working in Chaotung as the only surgeon for hundreds of miles around, where the Chinese doctors hung upon is every word and move, Frank realised that this unforeseen opportunity to gain actual hands-on experience could not have come at a better time. It meant that, in future work overseas, he would be able to undertake almost any type of operation with confidence. Thus began eighteen months as

Surgical Registrar in General Surgery at Southmead Hospital, Bristol. Having now discovered some of the problems and shortages with which he would be confronted abroad, Frank was able to prepare himself much more objectively for any future work overseas.

One other wonderful thing about this appointment was the fact that Frank was working with Mr. Capper, a renowned Gastric Surgeon, who taught him a great deal about Gastroenterology in general.

A Surgical Registrar in 1949/50 often worked very long hours and when 'on call' could be away from home for two or three days at a stretch. During this period we were living in a flat on Downleaze, a very pleasant area in Bristol on the downs near the Gorge. This was a distance of about three miles from Southmead Hospital and Frank's mode of transport to and fro was a sit-up-and-beg bicycle to which he fitted a small motor on the back wheel, which ran on petrol mixed with a little oil. He cannot now remember the exact mixture or where he obtained the oil. Anyway, he travelled much more quickly with the motor than without it.

Our flat was situated on the third floor of one of the lovely, large houses, which stood on Downleaze facing an area of open grassland. Across the expanse of grass, directly opposite the flat, was the Zoo, to which the entrance fee was just a few pence. I was able to spend many happy afternoons taking Rosemary in her pushchair to visit Rosie the elephant. Another favourite walk from the flat took us to the famous Bristol Suspension Bridge, with its magnificent view down to the river hundreds of feet below. Blackboy Hill was also within easy reach, very convenient for our day-to-day shopping, including buying bananas for Rosemary when the ship came in from Jamaica. Believe it or not, bananas were still rationed in 1950/51 and were reserved for young children only.

We lived on Downleaze for about eighteen months and during that time Rosemary grew from a baby to a delightful little girl. We had our exciting moments. One particular incident comes to mind, which Rosemary may just remember, when she bolted herself into the bathroom. As we were living high up on the third floor, we had to call the Fire Brigade to come to the rescue. The firemen set up a ladder against the outside wall of the house, climbed up, squeezed through the small bathroom window, which mercifully was open, unbolted the door from the inside and then, within a moment, Rosemary was free. Throughout the whole episode Rosemary remained quite unperturbed. Her little fingers had been strong enough to push the bolt to on shutting the door, but not to pull it open again.

There was no central heating in the flat. Electric heaters were available but they were expensive to run. It was cheaper to burn a coal fire in the lounge. Unfortunately the coal was stored in the cellar of the house and this meant hauling it up four flights of steps every day. This was one of my tasks because Frank spent very long hours away, working at the hospital. I must confess that, after becoming pregnant, I found this job rather daunting as I suffered quite badly with sciatica from mid-January onwards.

Frank was gaining masses of medical and surgical experience, which would stand him in good stead for our next posting abroad. We spent a good deal of time debating about our next venture abroad, especially as we should be taking two small children with us.

Eventually, very early on the morning of 20th June 1951, Jennifer was born. Frank was on duty at Southmead Hospital. It so happened that there were two Dr. Toveys' on the staff and when a telephone message was sent about Jenny's arrival it was put through to the Dr. Tovey who was soundly sleeping, as he was off-duty.

Needless to say, he was not best pleased to be woken from his well-earned slumber at two o'clock in the morning, but he did immediately contact Frank with the news and his congratulations.

The family together at Jenny's christening.

Zettie (Auntie Irene's paid companion), Irene Tovey, Ernest Tovey
Nellie Tovey, Frank, Rosemary, Jenny, Winnie, Nellie Hill, John Tovey

Shortly after Jenny's birth we heard from Mission House that there was an opening for Frank in the Holdsworth Memorial Hospital, Mysore City, South India. Holdsworth Hospital was established in 1906 for women and children only. In 1950, the Indian Nurses' Training Authority decreed that all hospitals with nursing schools for State Registered nurses must provide experience in nursing both male and female patients, and in caring for those who had undergone general surgery. We were quite excited about this job offer, as it would be a big challenge for Frank.

We accepted the position, and in mid-August 1951 a new chapter in our lives began. We set sail from Southampton on the P & O liner 'Chusan'.

In China after September 1949

The news of what happened in the two years following the Communist takeover ('Liberation') in September 1949 is of necessity second hand and consequently in places our account may not be truly accurate.

During the latter part of our stay in Chaotung four pleasant young men used to visit us of an evening to have tea. They were teachers, recently arrived in the town, who had called on us 'for conversation to improve their English'. Later we heard that in fact they were the advance party of the cadres appointed to set up a Communist regime in Chaotung. We were told that they were responsible for setting up Neighbourhood or Street Groups.

These Groups had to meet nightly for discussion and indoctrination, and each member of the Group had to prepare a life history, seeking the help of others if illiterate. In their life history they had to record all the major events of their lives, to explain why they did this or that, or why they thought one way or another. Then, every evening, their life histories were gone over in turn and the Group questioned their reasoning and thinking. In this way lists were compiled of (a) people amenable to Communism, (b) people who needed more indoctrination, and (c) those who would be resistant or reactionary. Those put in the second group were sent to indoctrination classes either nearby or far away, and those in the third group were eliminated. Often this was a call in the night and the person would never be heard of again.

Many people were denounced by their neighbours, then there would be public accusations, followed by imprisonment and often a firing party. Children were encouraged to denounce their parents, and to listen and report if they heard them saying anything counter-revolutionary.

Frank, one of the nurses, Winifred Sanders, and Rev Ken Parsons left just four days before the Communist takeover of Chaotung on September 3rd, but another nurse and one of the 'Women's Workers' decided to remain in Chaotung, as did Rev Vernon Stone, who had recently returned to China, leaving his family at home in England.

In June 1950 the group in Chaotung were joined by three more people; Rev Elliott (Dick) Kendall, another woman worker, an agriculturist who had came across from Weining, and Dr Dorothy Galbraith, who returned to the Chaotung Hospital, from her retirement, determined to continue working there until forced to leave.

Later in June 1950 every house in Chaotung city was searched and two hundred people were imprisoned. In the loft of the Hospital House the Communists discovered some long-forgotten spare radio parts and they accused the women workers of operating a radio transmitting station. A tense time followed. There were great risks in staying put, but also unknown dangers in leaving with no travel permits and the possibility of capture or worse on the road.

Eventually, in February 1951 Elliott Kendall and Vernon Stone left Chaotung for Kunming. When they arrived in Kunming, Vernon was imprisoned on the basis of having operated an illicit radio. Elliott stayed in Kunming to try to obtain his release.

While imprisoned, Vernon was fed two meagre meals a day and subjected to long, night time interrogations that consisted of hint and suggestion, plea and threat, rather than direct accusation. Suddenly, without explanation, Vernon was released in early July, and he and Elliott were escorted to Chungking, down the river Yangtze to Hankow, then by train to Canton and onwards to the border with Hong Kong, where they were eventually released to freedom.

At the same time, the nurse and a Woman Worker, who had remained in Chaotung, were evacuated by plane to Chungking. Earlier on, Dr Dorothy Galbraith, along with a retired missionary called Miss Squires, and two other Women Workers, had travelled by road to Kunming and then by plane to Hong Kong. From Hong Kong they were able to return to England and to recover from difficult times.

After this very little news came out of China and we tried not to dwell too much on our anxieties for friends and colleagues we had left behind.

Many years later we learnt more about events of the Communist Revolution. At first landlords were made to give up all their property and the land was shared out according to the number of people in a family or village, with the original landlord receiving one share. Later, however, landlords were regarded as enemies of the people and they were deprived of all rights and any livelihood. Some landlords were executed. Whole families starved and many were shot. Later the land was taken away from the peasants and collective farms (Cooperatives) were set up.

People in businesses were compelled to carry on as normal until they became bankrupt and then the State took over. The same happened to the Hospital.

We learnt that our language teacher, Rev John Li, aged 71 at the time of his arrest, was imprisoned and died while in prison, probably of typhoid. Our Medical Superintendent, Dr Nieh, was of the Nosu tribe. The Nosu people were landlords and therefore hated. His two brothers were shot and after this he shot himself. Dr Wang was enlisted into the Communist army. Two of the senior Chinese Christian Ministers hanged themselves because they could not withstand further interrogations.

We were told that the leprosy patients at Stone Gateway fled to the hills. Messages were sent out and they were encouraged to come back. Then after their return, one

Sunday morning when they were gathered in the church, the Communists set fire to the building and shot them as they ran out of the flames.

Over the decades of the Communist Revolution the world did not know what went on. The publication in 1992 of Jung Chang's book 'The Wild Swans' was an eye opener. In an interview for The Daily Telegraph, Jung Chang said, 'In terms of the big civilisations, China is unique in having no religions. If you have no God, no absolute power to answer, then your moral code is that of society. If society is upside down, so is your moral code.'

1980 onwards

In 1980 Frank met the first delegation of Chinese Gastroenterologists to visit the UK after the Cultural Revolution, and we were invited to visit China on a combined research and lecture tour in 1981 and again in 1984. Earlier research in India had shown that the prevalence of duodenal ulceration was greater in the wetter rice-eating areas of South India than in the drier wheat-eating areas of the North. The itineraries were so arranged to see if the same differences were present in China. The first visit covered areas in the south where the diet was mostly rice-based, and the second visit the drier areas in the north where wheat and different millets formed the staple diet.

These were early days of China opening again to the world and our movements were strictly planned. At all times we were escorted by a member of the Bureau of Health, an interpreter and a professor from the local hospital, and the places we visited were carefully chosen. In 1981 we found that there had been no contact with the West for 30 years, no foreign medical journals had been received, and everyone was anxious to catch up with developments that had taken place during this time. The lecture rooms were crowded to capacity.

Only the older people knew English and the younger ones were eager to learn. Everywhere one went in the larger cities there were loud speakers giving English lessons. During the Cultural Revolution all the senior doctors in the hospitals had been sent to the countryside to do community service and the hospitals were staffed by junior doctors.

The senior Professor of Medicine of one of the main hospitals we visited in Beijing was 82 years old. During the Cultural Revolution he had to clean the latrines in the hospital, using shards of broken glass to clean the lavatory pans. Medical education had suffered. After 1978 the senior doctors had been recalled and they were busy re-establishing standards of education.

In 1981, the wide streets of Beijing were thronged by men and women, in identical blue 'Mao suits', all walking or riding bicycles. There were no cars, except for the occasional official car, and no petrol pumps. Indeed the only pumps were those held by old ladies sitting on boxes on the pavements with bicycle pumps and repair kits waiting for customers with punctures! Likewise there were no car parks, only bicycle parks. The shops had no window displays, but there would be a notice above the door saying that it sold books or whatever.

In Hankow, the familiar streets near the Methodist Hospital where we first worked, still had the same flagstones, but the channel down to the river was covered and they were free of the sight and smell of excrement. We visited the Hospital and were welcomed by Dr Chiang who was Medical Superintendent when we were there in 1948.

Wherever we went, there was no unemployment. All work was labour intensive. Most people worked in Communes, which provided security as well as housing, albeit with whole families living in a single room and sharing kitchens and toilets. The Communes had their own hospitals and medical treatment was free. Old people were cared for.

Unfortunately we were not able to go to Chaotung because the rain had washed mudslides over the road, but in 1982 we had met a doctor from Chaotung and she told us about Chaotung Hospital at that time.

The original Mission Hospital of 40 beds was taken over by the Government in February 1951. More recently the new hospital of 400 beds, called the Chaotung District People`s Hospital was built on the site.

The new hospital has many departments, employs 470 workers, and caters for 280,000 outpatients and 13,000 inpatients a year.

As you will read in the pages to follow, 'The environmental health conditions in towns and villages has been greatly improved, and the level of hygiene and health of the people has been progressively lifted'.

Chaotung District People's Hospital 1982.

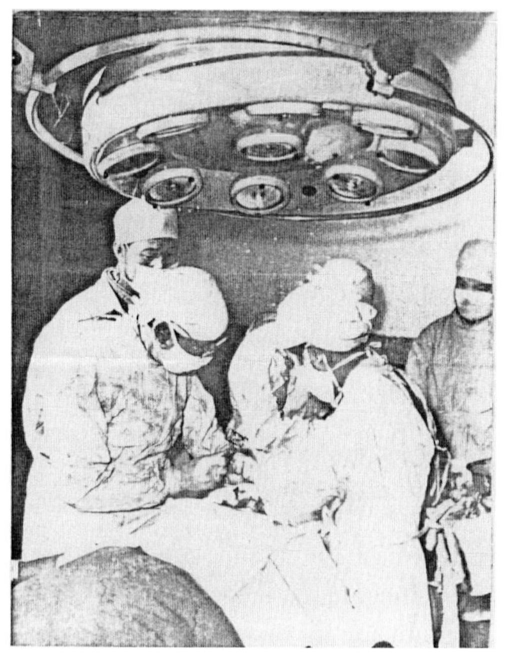

Chaotung District People's Hospital – view of wards and operating theatre.

1. CHAOTUNG DISTRICT PEOPLE'S HOSPITAL

When the People's Government took over the management of the Fuh Tien Hospital, Chaotung, in February, 1951, the name was changed to Chaotung District People's Hospital. The original hospital of only 40 beds has been expanded over the succeeding years, so that today there are 400 beds. The work is divided as follows :-

Surgical
1 General surgery
2 Orthopaedic surgery
3 Pulmonary, urological, brain-tumour
4 Brain, eye, ear, nose and mouth
5 Gynaecology
6 Maternity

Medical
1 gastro-enterology, neurology
2 cardiology, kidney, lungs

Paediatric clinic
Isolation ward
Chinese herbal treatment ward
Technical Department - radio-therapy equipment including deep X-ray treatment room
Pharmacy, including preparation of antibiotics
Laboratory
Pathology department
Ultrasonic diagnosis, including ultrasonic cardiograph room
Electro-encephalograph room
Cardiograph room
Acupuncture room
Casualty (emergency surgery) room
Blood bank

All clinical and surgical departments are well equipped. The technical department is equipped with X-ray apparatus, deep X-ray treatment apparatus, microscopes, colour scanner, multi-purpose examination apparatus, cardiographic apparatus, cardio-oscilloscope, electro-encephalograph apparatus, breathing apparatus in various sizes.

There are five well-equipped operating theatres, capable of performing head, brain, neck, chest, heart, gastro-intestinal, urological, eye, ear nose, mouth maternity and orthopaedic operations.

The hospital employs 470 workers, of whom 239 are doctors or nurses. Each year 280,000 out-patients are treated and 13,000 in-patients admitted.

Attached are photographs of
1. out-patients department
2. in-patients wards
3. an operating theatre

.... over

2. REPORT ON THE DEVELOPMENT OF HEALTH CARE IN THE CHAOTUNG DISTRICT

The medical and health care in the Chaotung District, like that of all other districts, is under the guidance of the People's Government. Due to the efforts of the past 30 years, the situation has been greatly changed from being small-scale, lacking in workers, poorly equipped, unable to cope with epidemics, to a modern medical service.

Up to the end of 1981, there are 12 epidemic prevention centres, 12 health centres for mothers and babies, 5 laboratories, 122 rural commune clinics, and 1,068 hospital beds in the district.

Skills and equipment for treatment and surgery are well developed. Most commune clinics have X-ray apparatus, shadowless surgical lamps, refrigerators, and gastro-intestinal instruments enabling abdominal surgery to be carried out there. A college in the district can teach medical care skills up to intermediate grade to many new workers.

In rural and remote areas production companies have established co-operative clinics. At the end of 1981 there are 925 co-operative clinics in the district, and 1,940 barefoot doctors. 467 workers, of whom 24.1% are barefoot doctors, have passed the intermediate grade examination and been granted the certificate of Rural Doctor. There are 1,260 health workers among the production companies, and 1,283 rural midwives.

In these ways the first steps have been taken to satisfy the needs of the masses for healing and preventive medicine. The environmental health conditions in towns and villages have obviously improved, and the level of hygiene and health of the people has been progressively lifted.

Yunnan Province, Chaotung District,
People's Hospital
2nd.June,1982

So it can be seen that out of greatly restricted and difficult times in China, some good things have emerged. At the time of writing, China, like the rest of the world, faces new challenges in social order, demographics, economics, globalisation, and management of natural and human resources. It remains to be seen how the country's resilient people will shape their future.

Glossary

aya - the name given to a children's nanny in India.

bandits - lawless people who raided and robbed travellers.

bloomers - voluminous women's or girls' underpants, usually gathered with elastic at the waist and legs.

Boxer Rebellion - an anti-imperialist, anti-Christian movement active from 1898 to 1901. In 1900 the Boxers attacked Mission compounds across north China.

Bund - an embankment or causeway

cable /telegram - the sending of urgent messages by radio transmission using Morse code to spell out the words.

camp bed - a transportable fold-out bed made from wood and canvas.

chin - Chinese for 'please'.

China Inland Mission - the non-sectarian China Inland Mission, founded by Hudson Taylor in 1865, from the beginning recruited missionaries from the working class as well as single women, encouraging them to adopt Chinese clothing and work and live close to the Chinese. On principles of faith and prayer the CIM sought to evangelise the whole of China while giving priority to unreached inland provinces. In 1964 the mission was renamed the 'Overseas Missionary Fellowship'. For more information search Wikipedia for 'OMF International'.

coolie - in China or India, a man whose main job was to carry goods, baggage or building materials.

DDT - the insecticide powder (dichlorodiphenyltrichloroethane) was in extensive use up to the early 1960s when there was concern over its environmental impact.

fag - slang for a cigarette.

furlough - a scheduled break from service overseas. Most missionaries would have one year back in England after five years practising abroad.

gangway - the removable steps or ramped bridge from a ship to the dockside.

Han Chinese - the ethnic majority peoples of China.

harmonium - a transportable musical reed organ, often with manual or foot-operated bellows.

hwa gan - carrying litter made of two long poles (usually bamboo) with stiffening rods and strong cloth or canvas between, carried on the shoulders of two men - a bit like a stretcher.

li - a measure of distance, 3 li equal 1 mile (the number of li are more uphill and less downhill).

Liberty bodice - a garment of female underwear, considered essential in Edwardian times and later, to keep the chest warm.

magic lantern - an old type of projector.

Methodist - a branch of the Protestant church started by the English West Country brothers, Charles and John Wesley.

Miao - an ethnic minority tribe of south China, (previously, often serfs to the Nosu).

Moravian - a branch of the Protestant church formed in Bohemia in 1457, and brought to the UK in the 1760's.

Nosu - an ethnic minority group from south China, traditionally landlords.

pothole - the hollow worked into a roadway by traffic passing over a badly maintained surface.

shorthand typing - a rapid writing code and touch typing, essential skills for a secretary or reporter before the days of word processors and PCs.

Special Licence - permission to marry within a shorter period than normally required for the reading of bans (the announcement for successive Sundays of a forthcoming marriage in church).

stook - a bundle of cut cereal stalks, straw or hay, often stacked in small piles to allow the crop to dry in the field before winnowing (separating the grain from the stalks).

swallet hole - a hollow or hole formed in the ground by the sinking of soil after soluble minerals below are washed away by rain and moisture.

Valedictory Service - a farewell church service held before a departure.

water carrier - in China, the man whose job it was to fetch water and carry it back to the house.

Strangers in Chaotung - list of illustrations

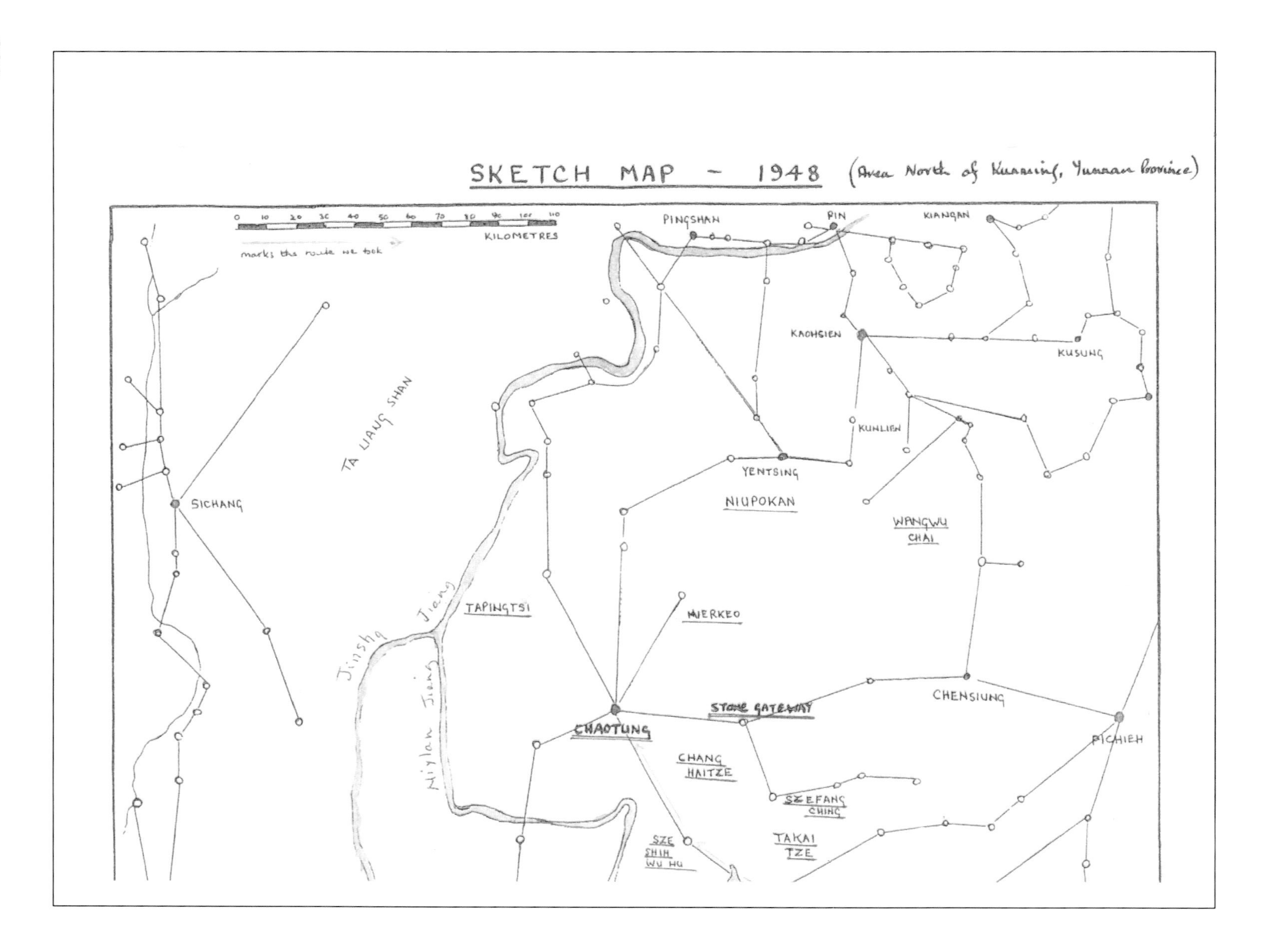
SKETCH MAP – 1948 (Area North of Kunming, Yunnan Province)
0 10 20 30 40 50 60 70 80 90 100 110
KILOMETRES
marks the route we took
PINGSHAN
PIN
KIANGAN
KAOHSIEN
KUSUNG
KUNLIEN
YENTSING
NIUPOKAN
WANGWU CHAI
SICHANG
TA LIANG SHAN
TAPINGTSI
WERKEO
Jinsha Jiang
Niulan Jiang
CHAOTUNG
STONE GATEWAY
CHENSIUNG
PICHIEH
CHANG HAITZE
SZEFANG CHING
TAKAI TZE
SZE SHIH WU HU